For Your Tomorrow,
We Gave Our Today

For Your Tomorrow, We Gave Our Today

A Memoir

Martin Maxwell

Centennial College Press
Toronto, Ontario
2024

Centennial College Press
951 Carlaw Avenue
Toronto, ON M4K 3M2

Mailing address
Centennial College Press
P.O. Box 631, Station A
Toronto, ON M1K 5E9

https://centennialcollegepress.com/

Copyright © 2024 by the Estate of Martin Maxwell.

All rights reserved. No part of this publication may be reproduced, distributed, or transmitted in any form or by any means, including photocopying, recording, or other electronic or mechanical methods, without the prior written permission of the publisher, except in the case of brief quotations embodied in critical reviews and certain other noncommercial uses permitted by copyright law. For permission requests, write to the publisher at the address above.

Cover photographs are courtesy of the author's estate.

For Your Tomorrow, We Gave Our Today is a memoir. It represents the late author's best recollection of events in which he participated or which he observed, and is meant as a contribution to history, though it is not a work of academic history itself. It should also be noted that the airborne operation in which Mr. Maxwell participated on D-Day was actually Operation Mallard, which was a follow-up to Operations Deadstick and Tonga intended to maintain the Allied capture of Pegasus Bridge.

Centennial College Libraries assisted the Press in the publication of this book.

Proofreaders: Elizabeth Sheldon and Riley Williamson

Contents

FOREWORD
by Dr. Ken Hedges
vii

INTRODUCTION
1

CHAPTER ONE
A Happy but Tragic Childhood
3

CHAPTER TWO
Rising Tensions
17

CHAPTER THREE
A New Start
25

CHAPTER FOUR
Historic Missions
37

CHAPTER FIVE
Liberation
49

CHAPTER SIX
Return to Civilian Life
67

CHAPTER SEVEN
Sharing My Experiences
73

AFTERWORD
A Visit to Vienna
89

ACKNOWLEDGEMENTS
93

A SELECTION OF PHOTOGRAPHS
AND DOCUMENTS
99

Foreword
by Dr. Ken Hedges

When you go home, tell them of us and say
For your tomorrow, we gave our today.
—*John Maxwell Edmonds (1875–1958),
Epitaph, Kohima War Cemetery*

"Dad never spoke about the war." How often has that been our experience? And why is that so often the case? In the aftermath of the American Civil War, General William Tecumseh Sherman offered a terse response: "War is hell." There is a moral ambiguity on the field of battle where the currency is bloodshed and body counts and territorial dominance, as opposing forces pit violence against violence. There is no immunity, only commitment and sacrifice as the consequences of conflict unravel to sometimes reveal man's better angels.

Max was my hero. Not because he was as tough as an old boot (although the battle-scarred evidence of old wounds and his quiet presence conveyed a very real sense of credibility). But because he was a man of honour.

In my experience there can be few circumstances in which personal integrity is more closely held or sternly tested than in the profession of arms. Indeed, it is the presence of honourable men and women, their accountability to their sovereign and their conscience, that ensures that our armed forces will not conduct our nation's affairs outside the honourable traditions of a call to the colours.

On the face of it, it seemed unlikely that Max and I would ever have crossed paths. He was my senior by eleven years. We spoke different languages. Max had been raised in Vienna and since I had spent my early childhood years in Fiji, we had literally lived half a world apart. He was orphaned, stateless and held no passport. He was Jewish and I was not.

We were to meet over half a century later. That evening, as Max addressed his audience at the Royal Canadian Military Institute, there was something about the speaker which demanded attention. He spoke quietly and with disarming candour. This was no researched historical re-telling of battles won and lost. This was the testimony of a witness to the horrors and cost of unconditional warfare.

What was it that these brave souls might experience as they confronted a waiting enemy? Hypervigilance, shock, fear, grief, anger exhaustion, confusion and the pervading presence of exposure to environmental extremes or some other uninvited affliction? All that … and the risk of indiscriminate violence. They would be quick to acknowledge that although they acted and reacted individually, they did not act alone as fate cast its shadow upon their line of advance. They might sense a wave of unsettling emotion surging from deep within their skulls. Yet they stood their ground, reminding themselves of their orders, perhaps finding comfort in each other's presence, perhaps realizing because of the drumbeat of military training and proven leadership that duty called, that marching orders had been heard, understood and acknowledged. They hunkered down, counting themselves ready, willing and able to meet the expectation of their mates and to sense their encouragement.

Born and raised within a loving but impoverished family and in an era of pervasive anti-Semitism, Max Meisels grew up to become a tough young street kid. He was to develop a resilience forged by his Jewish legacy and a resourcefulness forged out of grim necessity.

As I reflected upon the legacy within the warp and weft of Max's story, there was a recurring theme of uncompromising audacity. Chutzpah: it is an enigmatic Aramaic term that, as explained by Lord Jonathan Sacks, was introduced into the Hebrew language at the time of the Assyrian invasion and mass deportation of the small vassal kingdom of Judah to Babylon around 605 BCE. Max stood before his audience as a man of purposeful daring, a man who took calculated risks not so much for personal advantage but arising from "an informed heart" (a concept found in Holocaust survivor and professor of psychology Bruno Bettelheim's analysis on "Surviving") and intended for the betterment of others.

In the lead-up to the Second World War (1939–1945), there was an insidious climate of ideological aggression at play: Stalin in Russia. Hitler in Germany. Franco in Spain. Mussolini in Italy. Tojo in Japan. For most unaffected observers, the easiest thing to do was to look the other way. But that was to present a debilitating mindset of indifference to the consequences of oppression. It was this wishful thinking of appeasement which was to present fertile ground for the voracious momentum of tyranny against a demoralized opposition.

It is said that today that Jews make up just one quarter of one percent of our entire global population. Yet not for the first time, and on this occasion within my own lifetime, the Jewish peoples had become the targeted victim of a deliberate and cruel violence as the rhetoric of Nazi Germany took aim with a driven hatred upon their contrived enemy. Thus the mass murder of Jews, nothing less than genocide, became embedded within the mythology of the German Third Reich under the tyranny of Hitler.

Max and his cohort came to represent the remnants of European Judaism in the aftermath of a brutal conflagration and the near extinction of European Jewry. The Holocaust—nurtured in the prevailing anti-Semitic stereotypes of the day; spring-triggered by the unopposed hatred of organized collaborators within the Nazi party; and nurtured by the comfortable indifference of countless bystanders.

Max of necessity would change his name. He concealed his own Jewish identity so that voiceless victims of Nazi brutality might regain their personhood, to no longer be recorded solely as a degrading concentration camp number tattooed upon their emaciated bodies.

To my mind, of the many obligations recorded within the scrolls of the Hebrew Bible, few words better express Captain Martin Maxwell's mindset than a Mitzvah (command) recorded in the book of Leviticus, chapter 19, verse 16:

"Do not stand idly by while your neighbour's life is threatened."
(New Living Translation).

Among the German-speaking peoples, the fractured vitriol of dictatorship had served to instil an idea of entitlement, breeding a loathing for any who stood in the way of their fabricated self-image. There was a lust for revenge against those countries that had won the First World War (1914–1918) with their imposed indignities and suffocating reparations. Now their weakness appeared to be no match for the organized forces of military dictatorships. On offer was the rewarding prospect of expansive colonialism with plundered resources and forced labour.

The prospect of universal justice was no longer at play. There emerged a tsunami of politically inspired vindictiveness as the coercive effects of social marginalization became industrialized. Sanctioned violence percolated all levels of bureaucracy. Murder squads were raised. Concentration camps (first devised by the British during the Boer War) now added the gruesome expectation of death by disease or starvation. Dedicated extermination camps such as Auschwitz offered a ghoulish and more efficient mechanism of murder in which victims, having first been asphyxiated by Zyklon B, were then incinerated. No one was safe, no one immune, almost no one escaped.

Yet Max saw the good and not just the bad among innocent German citizens and especially their children. His critique of the pervasive fascist bestiality which coloured his early life was not lacking a note of conciliation for decent people caught on the wrong side of history. Following the war's end, as a German-speaking officer in the British Army working under the auspices of the Nuremberg War Crimes Tribunal, he would seek out the guilty, but would never wield the cudgel of shame against innocent Germans who themselves had become part of the collateral damage of war. In this, Max would echo the words of Fritz Rodeck, whose essay was included in Harvard sociologist Edward Hartshorne's book *Night of Broken Glass*, which dealt with the aftermath of the November 9/10, 1938, pogrom we have come to know as Kristallnacht:

> Our non-Jewish neighbours were all ashamed and deeply depressed, and one got the impression that they had a guilty conscience and feared the power of a higher justice.... These people saved, as much as that was still possible, the honour of the German people.

Offshore in the North Atlantic Ocean stood a small group of islands, the United Kingdom of Great Britain and Northern Ireland. The UK and its inhabitants had tolerated a modicum of Sir Oswald Mosley's fascism. They were only separated from the warring factions of Europe by a strait (the English Channel) that was narrow enough one could see the other side. It was, however, just wide enough to present a barely sufficient obstacle to the advancing Nazi legions of Hitler's Third Reich.

But the Brits had something going for them which any adversary would have been hard-pressed to match. They rallied around a new

King, George VI, and his family, who were instinctively dedicated to their sovereign peoples. Britain enjoyed an unquestioned sense of historic fellowship with the Commonwealth of Nations, and in particular the dominions of Australia, Canada, New Zealand, and South Africa. And most of all, as an ill-prepared nation reeling from the opening setbacks and shocks of conflict, they were to become quickly attuned to the unique geopolitical grasp and inspired oratory of a battle-hardened old warrior, Winston Churchill.

It was Churchill who was to set the parameters when he drove home to a bewildered and discouraged British public the unconditional demands of warfare which now confronted them:

> You ask, what is our policy? I can say: It is to wage war, by sea, land and air, with all our might and with all the strength that God can give us; to wage war against a monstrous tyranny, never surpassed in the dark, lamentable catalogue of human crime. That is our policy. You ask, what is our aim? I can answer in one word: It is victory, victory at all costs, victory in spite of all terror, victory, however long and hard the road may be; for without victory, there is no survival.

We're in for a roller coaster of a ride in the pages ahead as we're carried within earshot of the tragedy of war through the eyes of a Jewish orphan and refugee, later a feisty young soldier and latterly the man whose life story we shall be hard pressed to ever forget. His narrative includes his involvement in Operation Mallard, which saw Allied gliders land in occupied France. This was a follow-up to Operation Deadstick, in which six Horsa gliders, each packed with 30 fighting men, descended on the French coastline during the early morning hours of D-Day in ghostly silence like predatory owls in search of prey. Their mission: to take and hold Pegasus Bridge, securing the left flank of the Allied bridgehead.

For Your Tomorrow, We Gave Our Today

They had flown aloft on a wing and a prayer. Some would make it. Some would not. In the hand-to-hand fighting that followed, this small band was to suffer what are believed to have been the first two Allied deaths on D-Day. One lad drowned when his glider landed in a swamp. The rest of the assault party advanced undetected until reaching the bridge six hours before the landings on the Normandy beaches. The young officer leading the charge was mortally wounded. In the calculus of battle, two men killed in action was an acceptable rate of attrition, for with the element of surprise—and a necessary exercise of chutzpah—they had achieved their objective. The soldiers troops involved in Operation Mallard were tasked with reinforcing the earlier attack and making sure the Allies held onto their hard-won gains. (In his memoir, written from memory long after the fact, Max conflates the two related operations.) But this exhilarating victory had been achieved on the shoulders of their fallen comrades. They would not be forgotten. There was a respectful sadness as they awaited an inevitable Wehrmacht counterattack. Air Chief Marshall Sir Trafford Leigh-Mallory characterized the D-Day glider operations, so remarkable in terms of flying skill, navigational precision, and tactical initiative, as "one of the most outstanding flying achievements of the war."

Max's account of his life is not sugar-coated, for like the prophet Jeremiah, the lessons he draws from the tragedy of war will echo: "You cannot heal a wound by saying it isn't there." Yet as an agent of hope, his story extends beyond World War II as he warns of dangers ahead. The same dangers which, unknown to Max at the time, had forcefully taken the innocent lives of two of his little sisters as they disappeared into the ugly maw of Nazi atrocities. The same subtle dangers which some 1,700 black American troops experienced on the D-Day beachhead when there was no mention of their presence because of insidious racial prejudice.

D-Day was for Max a springboard for a life that would later

include both grievous and exhilarating challenges. Ours is the last generation that will be privileged to receive a firsthand account of the sacrifices, resilience and service of Max's generation. As Max put his experiences down on paper, he confided how he slept only fitfully as he was painfully reminded of his own family losses and of his witness to the horrors of warfare. It remained a price which he and his devoted wife Eleanor were willing to pay in order that we might hear directly from this extraordinarily brave Jewish war veteran.

Max passed away in 2020. Captain Martin Maxwell had been appointed a Chevalier (Knight) in the French Legion d'Honneur in grateful recognition of his role on D-Day. His work has been cited in the Canadian Parliament and he is a recipient of the Queen Elizabeth Diamond Jubilee medal for his service to Canada.

Sadly the nature of Max's indisposition prevented his attendance at what was to be his final Remembrance Day. Even so, his spirits were lifted when the British High Commissioner accompanied by her Defence Adviser and Naval and Air Adviser sent a personal video expressing their appreciation of Max's wartime service from the cenotaph in Ottawa to his hospital bed. His eyes sparkled.

I'm glad he was on our side.

Ken Hedges is best known as a member of the British Trans-Arctic Expedition, which reached the North Pole by dog sled in 1969 as part of a 5,987-kilometre journey from Alaska to Norway. Hedges graduated from the University of Liverpool's medical school in 1962 and served in the Royal Army Medical Corps and the British Special Air Service. After immigrating to Canada in 1975, he served as a major in the Canadian Forces Medical Service (Reserve) and held various administrative positions before resuming clinical practice in 1982. He passed away at the age of 88 in October 2023.

For Your Tomorrow,
We Gave Our Today

Introduction

May 5, 2020 was the 75th anniversary of the liberation of Holland. My plans to be in the Netherlands had been postponed indefinitely due to the invasive destruction of a different enemy—Covid-19. I did, however, travel there for the 60th anniversary of the liberation. One reason was to visit the Arnhem Oosterbeek War Cemetery, where the graves are faithfully tended to by the ever-grateful Dutch people; they will never forget. At this particular site, seventeen hundred of my own division as well as Poles and Americans lay buried. Of the ten thousand of us that came to Arnhem by glider or parachute on the 14th and 15th of September, 1944, to capture the bridge over the Rhine, only two thousand returned. The rest were killed, wounded, or taken prisoner.

All the ceremonies had been held in the morning, and when the editor of the local newspaper, my wife and I arrived, only five others were in attendance. As I slowly entered the section with the graves, I noticed the tall trees with their light green leaves swaying in the wind, back and forth, as if they were saluting and honouring those lying here in this sacred earth.

As I walked past the gravestones I thought about how young we all were: twenty, twenty-one. There were not many over twenty-two. I came to a corner and found the names John and David—a cross on one gravestone and the Star of David beside it. David was someone I remembered. He had come with me as a young refugee on the Kindertransport. We had such high hopes; we were going to be partners in some future venture. And I remembered John, too, from the glider pilots. He could tell the most wonderful jokes and stories and make us all laugh. Next to their graves was another that pulled at my heartstrings. No cross or Star of David—no name—just "Here Lies a Soldier." Are you here, my Welsh friend Evan, with your beautiful dream that, as a son of a miner, you would be the first in your family to get an education and become a doctor? We never found you but wherever you are, rest in peace. Our friendship was so short but intense. I have never forgotten you, and I never will.

"God gave us memory so that we might have roses in December." One memory I took home with me and will always keep is the verse, "When you go home tell them of us and say, / For your tomorrow, we gave our today." Thousands of young men and women were injured or gave their lives so future generations would live in freedom. Their lives, cut short by their bravery, were devoted to us. I somberly reflect on life today and ask, "What have *we* done with the tomorrows they gave us?" The struggle goes on.

My own early years presented me with many tribulations. The severe Depression of the 1930s, the hunger and hardship of those initial years in Vienna, and the early deaths of both my loving parents made me question my existence and purpose in life. Although I attended synagogue and studied the Torah, that was not the escape from reality that would forge my future life. I had to survive; and it was a combination of events and my own determination and optimism that gave me the will to do so. Along the way I found strength in the help of several others. My inherent personality and desire to socialize, along with a somewhat mischievous demeanour and positive outlook, led me into many situations that might have proved to be detrimental but usually concluded in some "saving grace" that was beneficial and humorous. I love to laugh at my own shortcomings, and I made many new friends in my early days and later in life. They are part of the story I tell in the pages ahead.

CHAPTER ONE

A Happy but Tragic Childhood

I was born Max Meisels on March 26, 1924, in Vienna, Austria. Prior to my birth, my parents moved from Poland (my mother from Tarnów, my father from Józefów) to Vienna due to the poor economic conditions ravaging Poland at the time. The lack of food and work sent many down the same path. Vienna, on the other hand, was a thriving cultural centre. Austria had been ruled by Emperor Franz Joseph I for over 67 years until his death in 1916, and his legacy was defined by his anti-nationalist views which resulted in policies that allowed Jews to flourish in professions such as law, medicine, banking and the arts. In 1918 approximately two-thirds of Austria's 300,000 Jews resided in Vienna, making it a central hub for Judaism in Europe.

Until I was five years old, I lived in the 16th District of Vienna as an only child. I never experienced any anti-Semitism during that time because there were no Jews in that neighbourhood, and being so young, I, of course, did not have the capability to understand much of the concept of religion in any case. One day I was out playing soccer in the street when one of the boys came up to me and said that my Mama and Papa wanted me to come home. When I arrived, I remember there was a strange man with a moustache wearing a bowler hat. My parents told me that he was my real father. I was at first bewildered, then upset and confused. My only memories were of these lovely people as my parents, and I as their only child.

I was told that when my parents moved from Poland to Vienna they could not find suitable accommodations for the whole family, so the government deemed that they were not fit to look after their children. I had been taken in by the people I thought were my real parents, and now they were telling me that I had to go with this strange man (but they would let me take my toys with me, as if they believed this would appease me). In my bewilderment and frustration, tears flooded my face as this tall, poorly dressed stranger took my hand and tried to soothe my fears. My sobs made me gasp as I stumbled along with him. The people I thought were my parents also cried when I left. The awkward-looking man held my suitcase, already packed with clothes and a few of my beloved toys; I remember it was hard to keep up because he took such long strides.

Would I ever again see my beloved first "Papa" and "Mama"? Why did they give me up without a fight? It took many years for me to comprehend that their love and devotion to me was insufficient to deal with government bureaucracy. They were as unprepared as I was to lose me. From the beginning of my care, they had undertaken to assist my family, and always knew it was a temporary arrangement—not under their control.

Did this first shock to me as a five-year-old prepare me for the harsh future I would face? I may have succumbed bitterly to my own anger and dismay, but even then, I felt the need to overcome adversity when it confronted me. My immediate pains were soothed by the comfort of a new loving family, who greeted me with no reservations. I gradually became attached to my new older brother, Leo (7 years old), who guided me and gave me confidence. My two younger sisters, Josephine (4) and Erna (2), were happy to have another older brother, but the impact of crowded, impoverished living conditions and scarcity of food made life difficult for all of us.

I found a great sense of strength in the love and devotion of my mother and father. I was determined at this young age to adjust to this different family life. I tried hard to take more responsibility for my family's welfare. Leo was not always at my side as he moved out to live at a nearby Yeshiva, which included room and board along with the study of our Jewish heritage and traditions. But I never forgot the beloved couple who lovingly took me in as a toddler, until my parents were able to move into a government-subsidized apartment. I was forbidden from trying to reach them, which was very painful for me.

We went to live in a new apartment built by the socialist government in the 10th District, on the outskirts of Vienna. The apartment had only two bedrooms and a kitchen, no toilet. The toilet was down the hall, shared with three other units. Bathing took place at the communal bath houses. The apartment was not in a Jewish area, and when we moved in a large crowd gathered because many had never seen a Jew before (the population of Vienna at the time was about two million). A boy around my age lived next door to us and he asked me to play soccer with him and the other boys. He was aptly called "Little Ricky" and he told his friends that although I was a Jew, I was a good kid so they had better not give me any problems.

In my new-found family, daily life was a struggle for all. Most of all, I felt the frustration of my father, Abraham, who tried each day to find work to keep our family barely fed. My mother, Rachel, was constantly scouring to keep our family clothed, clean and nourished while performing the ritual tasks of a Jewish mother. No matter what happened, she did her utmost for us to keep the Sabbath and for us to study and learn about our Torah and traditions.

Somehow, she always managed to have a Shabbat meal consisting of chicken soup, gefilte fish, and her handmade challah, and this was lovingly looked forward to by all of us. She also saved all week to put together a meal of cholent (stew) for the Sabbath the next day. I would deliver our pot to the communal oven (made of bricks and metal) where the Jewish households each placed their own pots with the meat, vegetables and beans on Friday to be baked and eaten on the day of rest (Saturday), to avoid cooking on the Sabbath. Once, there were five or six pots when I arrived on Saturday. Since my family was so big, I took the biggest pot. My mother scolded me, but our meal was plentiful! I often feel guilty about the poor family that was left short on food as a result, and had no choice but to take what was left—our meagre substitute.

Austria was (and still is) a Catholic country, so I was to attend a government-run Catholic school. This would be the first time I encountered anti-Semitism personally. As the single Jew in class, I was barred from attending the religious classes and would be sent to walk the hallways until the class was over. When I would return the kids would yell at me, saying I had murdered Jesus. I said I was only six years old, how could I have killed anybody? "Who is this Jesus?" I asked. Little Ricky stood up for me to the biggest bully, saying I was only a child and besides, Jesus died over 1930 years ago. He called the bullies stupid, which started a big fight. We were two tough kids, though, and after that the bullies left us alone for the most part. Ricky's father showed us how to protect ourselves with some basic boxing lessons, as well.

When I was six years old, my mother was sitting in a corner, knitting. I remember I fell down and my mother said, "Max, get up, come over here and I'll kiss it better." I think this small but stark memory has stuck with me for a reason. From that early memory, I learned that it's not so bad to fall down—you can always try to get back up.

One day at gym class, one of the boys told his friends that Jews can't eat ham and if they do they go straight to hell. They thought it would be funny to make me eat a ham sandwich. They threatened me and physically held me down. I was obviously hungry so I ate it, and I remember thinking it tasted good. I was afraid, however, that something might happen to me because I had been taught that I was not allowed to eat pork. I was scared for a few days afterwards, fearing I would go to hell. I started attending a Jewish school at the synagogue in the evenings after the Catholic school let out for the day, to learn what it meant to be Jewish. Also, every Saturday we would walk as a family for two miles to attend synagogue.

Despite my social troubles at school, I was a good student. My uncle (who was an accomplished stage actor in Vienna) gave me an album with some stamps in it, and I was eager to learn every city and country as well as their populations. I was always near the top of the class in history and geography, and I also played soccer well.

My father had health problems and therefore couldn't earn much money by working. On occasion, he was able to work and we would have some food. I would be lying in bed when he came home, and if there was money he would wake us so we could eat. I remember one time he woke me to give me some milk, but I was so tired that I spilled it all over the bed. I would go to the bread box, but there wouldn't even be crumbs. We did get some milk at school, though. One time I went with my sisters to visit the family with whom they had been placed. We were very hungry and they were happy to give us some food, but we were told not to visit again (due to the law). The people who lived next door to us knew that we didn't have much, and they would have me over to eat a few times a week. I remember once they gave me two wiener schnitzels but I said I couldn't eat both of them. They told me to take them home because it would be a sin to throw them away.

One day, we came home from school to find my mother wasn't there. We were told that she had gone to the hospital to have a baby. I didn't really understand what was happening but I remember exclaiming that we didn't have room for another person in the apartment. My sisters and I went to the hospital and yelled "Mother, we are hungry, we have nothing to eat!" Some windows opened and people threw rolls down so we had something for dinner. Eventually my mother brought the baby, my sister Berta, home to us.

Life in Vienna during the Depression was extremely difficult. For a struggling family of five, we could only depend on any part-time earnings my father could bring home each day for food. He waited for his turn every day to deliver parcels or messages for large companies. My determination to overcome the physical difficulties of the lack of food for my family made me concentrate on efforts to improve the situation. I tried to think of ways I might bring some money home that would help us.

Farmers' markets were open in the summer and they were very busy because everyone who could afford fresh food was there to purchase the meagre supplies. I noticed many people who worked hard, became quite thirsty and required a drink or two. Many major street intersections had central fountains or a well where drinking water was clean, free and available. I managed to find a long, sturdy wooden stick, placed it over my shoulders, and attached a pail of fresh water at each end. With two small cups, I was able to offer the water to anyone who wanted it. At the age of seven, I began my first business venture, calling out "Fresh water, only two groschen a glass!" The small change added up; by the end of a hot day, I may have accumulated up to a hundred and fifty groschen (pennies). Then, when the farmers began to close up, I would ask if they had any damaged fruit that I could purchase at a discount. This is how I was able to bring home some slightly damaged apples and pears, and had my first taste of a juicy watermelon slice and an orange!

One day on my way home, my stomach rumbled as I passed a Jewish bakery run by an elderly man. I coveted the delicious-looking Napoleon in the window, dripping with whipped cream, but decided a more practical purchase would be that of sustaining bread, even if stale, and I asked the gentleman (a Hungarian Jew) if he had any leftovers that I could purchase for my hungry family at home. He quickly realized that I desired quantity rather than freshness and kindly filled my bag not only with leftovers, but also with several fresh delights for my few pennies.

The next time I returned at the end of the day, he made me sit down and placed in front of me a fresh kaiser roll with cheese and a glass of lemonade. He insisted that I eat it right there and in addition, when I dug into my pocket to pay him my 50 groschen for a full bag of buns and bread, he refused to accept it, pointing to a small blue and white box. "Please put your money into this collection for the Jews in Palestine. This will help us achieve our own country where we won't be attacked by the anti-Semites that are becoming as violent here in Vienna as elsewhere across Europe!"

I became close friends with the baker and would visit him regularly. When I had a few pennies left over he asked me to place them in the blue and white box he had on the counter—he said the money was to buy trees in Palestine. He sorrowfully told me that he would probably never see Palestine, but that I might. He was right; his store would soon be destroyed by fire amid rising anti-Semitic tensions. Food became crumbs and ashes, and he was never seen or heard from again.

"I know the swastikas are here," he said, "but it's important to remember that one day we'll have a country of our own. But until then, remember this. We will have to fight for it and even when we have it, we'll have to continue fighting for it" (echoing the views of the Zionist leader Ze'ev Jabotinsky).

One Christmas Eve, I decided to walk to the affluent part of town and look at the decorations. One home in particular caught my eye, and I stared through the window at a Christmas tree that seemed to illuminate the whole house. The owners noticed me and asked if I would like to come in from the cold. Their son recognized me from school. They could see that I was Jewish and poor, as by this time I had grown payos (traditional Jewish sidelocks). I told them

I had three sisters, a brother, a mother and a cancer-stricken father. The lady left the room and returned with four small packages with my mother's first name written on them. Within the parcels was about 300 schillings, which was more money than I had ever seen in my life up to that point. By this time anti-Jewish sentiment was relatively strong in Vienna, but even in difficult times there were caring people who saw us as one and the same as they. I have never forgotten their kindness. I came back and visited the area years later, only to find that it had been completely destroyed in the war.

As I hurried along to my Cheder (a school for continuing Jewish education) each day after school, I passed many shops and outdoor displays. The first part of my walk was in the poorer Jewish neighbourhood, and the Great Depression made it very difficult for so many to eke out a living. Had I foreseen what would have become of these struggling Jewish families, my spirit to cope and my faithful optimism would likely have been overcome with despair.

The main street I walked along passed by many smaller roads and laneways. Horses and wagons were still in use as the cars wove in and out to avoid them. Piles of refuse cluttered the sidewalk and overspilled their rank contents close to the curb. I turned onto my Cheder's street, which was in the more upscale Jewish area. The houses were set apart, and especially our converted "schoolhouse." "I must hurry," I told myself, and I managed each day to arrive before the Shema (prayer) to take my place and be ready for the lesson.

The biblical stories of our revered heroes stirred my imagination. Although our family was following Orthodox traditions and kept kosher we were not as strictly religious as many other Jewish families. Normally the men attended Shabbat services at this same converted house; women, at home, usually did the cleaning and prepared meals. My father and I attended each Sabbath. If the women joined the men on special Holy Days they were allocated to the upstairs section along with the many younger children.

As I turned my attention to our daily portion of the Chumash (a Torah in printed and bound form) I often gazed at the rays of light through the side windows. It became almost an expected trial for the shul (synagogue) to replace windows repeatedly smashed by encroaching youths. No one would put a stop to it and the police and city officials turned a blind eye whenever Jewish property was deliberately destroyed.

My family attended a very small synagogue in Vienna. Every Saturday, hooligans would break windows at every small synagogue in town. The larger synagogues had members stationed outside on Saturdays to keep the gangs away, but smaller ones like ours were easy targets.

I eventually joined an organization involved with the Zionist movement (that also gave away sandwiches!). Members of the group asked why we let hooligans get away with vandalizing our sacred houses of worship. Then and there we decided to get all the Jewish kids in the 10th District together and protect the synagogues. Armed with clubs and sticks, our small force prepared to fight before the vandals could unleash their damage. When the hooligans arrived we beat them up, and as a result we enjoyed six weeks of respite from the attacks. The police, however, told our parents that they would be fined if we continued to fight, so we had to stop. I had learned another hard lesson: if I wanted to preserve my own deserved beliefs and my very life, I must fight to defend them.

Because I was the only student from our part of the lower working class area (the 10th District), I was often the subject of derision by some of the better-dressed and obviously more middle class young boys. In spite of this, I did make some chums as we all had to take our studies very seriously.

Our teacher was a stern elderly rabbi with a short gray beard, Rabbi Buchsbaum. The stiff wool of his jacket made him twist his neck and scratch his head quite often and this made us laugh. His son, Moishele, was also one of the students. The rabbi carried a long flat ruler, which he would make use of either on our backside or hand if any one of us was misbehaving or up to mischief. He usually began by his reading of a particular section; we reiterated and wrote it until we got it perfect. He would then call on any single student to give an interpretation of that section. Any lack of attention or smirks of mischief would not be tolerated.

Little Moishele, the rabbi's son, was most unpopular because he was the school "snitch." If any student's attention strayed from the lesson, due to boredom or daydreaming, perhaps hiding and reading from an unauthorized magazine, Moishele would immediately call his father: "Tata, look what he's doing!" Punishment was immediate.

As a group, the rest of us were united in getting even with Moishele. Some of the levity that amused me as a child helped me to endure many physical hardships. A sense of humour and a mischievous nature, not always at the appropriate time, allowed for a laugh or two.

On a particular day, late in the lesson, it was announced that a group of adults were coming to attend a special session after our instruction. They would be reading the sacred Torah scrolls in the sanctuary behind the altar for their prayers.

As our class quickly dispersed after Rabbi Buchsbaum left for personal reasons, several of us grabbed little Moishele and held him kicking and screaming as we put a tight cloth over his mouth. We tied up his legs and arms and hid him behind the large cabinet where the Torah scrolls were kept. On his return, the rabbi asked where his son was and we all announced that he had left to go home.

Shortly after, as the grown-ups entered, they began their service by taking out the sacred scrolls. Much to their shock and dismay, they beheld and immediately released the crying and disgruntled snitch. The rabbi, face red with anger, held his cane high demanding to know who the perpetrators were. As we all were in on it, no one individual was blamed and eventually the incident was overlooked. But Moishele never again reported to his father when we went mischievously astray. Each day, my one-hour walk home was a heavy burden but these minor humorous situations gave me thought for some diversion.

I continued to be teased at day school, particularly because of my payos (sideburns). One day I went to the barber and told him that my father had said to cut them off. The barber was reluctant to do so because he knew the significance of them, but I was persistent so eventually he relented. I went home knowing my father would be upset, and I asked my brother Leo what I should do. I told him the barber made a mistake and cut them off accidentally. Leo said to stay away from my father and maybe he wouldn't notice. From then on, I never grew payos again.

One thing I excelled at when I was young was singing. I used to sing in a big choir at a large synagogue, for which I was paid the equivalent of 25 cents a month. When people were called up to read from the Torah they would make a donation, part of which was supposed to be distributed to the choir members.

On other occasions, I was invited to a special larger synagogue in the 10th District on Quellenstrasse. Vienna was, at that time, home to many Jewish families and the most prominent synagogue was the Polish one. I loved to sing; I knew the most important prayers and liturgies in Hebrew and was even paid to perform in the choir. Often, for a wedding or notable occasion, I would come to this great synagogue and perform to the accompaniment of a notable pianist or violinist. Eagerly, I agreed to come as a sizable meal would be provided. The wealthier patrons made donations to the synagogue and a small portion was always dedicated to the choir. However, we never benefited from any donation and continued to perform for the equivalent of 25 cents a month (per singer). We soon bravely petitioned for our money, and threatened to go on strike just before

Rosh Hashanah if we did not receive our due. The board members agreed to a raise—to 50 cents a month.

There was a famous cantor from another synagogue, Cantor Weiss. Every Saturday I would walk three miles to get there, because I couldn't afford to take the streetcar (it cost maybe 20 cents). One day, the cantor told me there was to be a wedding in the evening and invited me to stay after services for lunch as time was too short for me to go home and then return to sing for the event. Of course I never turned down a meal, so I accepted. In what I considered to be a palatial house, the dining table was laden with such a variety and quantity of delicious courses that I could not contain my appetite and gorged on more than my small belly could absorb. In short order I became ill. I was taken to the hospital and had to have my stomach pumped. When I was asked by my host "Why did you eat so much?" my embarrassed response was that I hoped to stuff myself so that I would not feel hunger for an entire week. He generously packed up some leftovers for me to take to my family. This lesson may have served me well, as after my liberation from the POW camp we were sternly warned to eat only small amounts until our stomachs could gradually accept larger portions.

When I was nine, my father got tickets to see the famous cantor Yossele Rosenblatt at another synagogue, which was in the 2nd District where many Jews lived. This cantor was offered $1 million to sing at the opera and turned it down because he would have been committed to perform on Saturdays or religious holidays. People lined up to get the tickets and we could have sold them for a lot of money, but my father insisted that the two of us go. He said, "You'll never forget seeing this cantor sing," and I never did. He sang Hallel, and people were going crazy. He was like a rock star. I can still see the concert in my mind, everyone cheering and even crying. When it was over, everyone hugged and kissed each other. This was a highlight of my life, even to this day when I recall the event.

My uncle was an actor on the Yiddish stage, and he had a car. When he came to visit us, his was the only car on the street. When he found out that my father was sick, he decided he would take him on a trip. When my father came back a week or two later, he had oranges and other gifts for us that we had never seen before. I learned later that the reason he went on the trip was because he was so sick and close to death. Everyone in my immediate family died many years later of colon cancer, including Leo and Berta. My uncle died a few years after my father, also from colon cancer.

My father continued to suffer from an aggressive cancer. I remember him crying from the pain, but we could not afford any of the medicine he needed. In 1935, when I was eleven, my father succumbed to his illness. I remember having my first argument with G–d as I walked behind my father's coffin. I did my homework, prayed regularly, and did whatever I could to help my family out. What had I done to deserve this? The people in our apartment building took pity on us when he passed; I remember they made soup for us and ensured that it did not contain any pork.

My mother couldn't care for us on her own so we were sent to Jewish orphanages. My sisters went to a small Jewish orphanage in Vienna and I was to go to a different one located in Baden. I remember Little Ricky walked me to the train station and promised me we would be friends forever. Ricky was eventually forced to join the army and spent time working in a concentration camp. He died fighting on the Russian front. When I returned to Vienna many years later, as an adult, I visited the building where I used to live. The people living in our unit (#38) wouldn't let us in to look even though I explained that my family had lived there many years ago. Perhaps they were suspicious that we wanted the sparse furniture that we had left behind. But an old man sitting there recognized me and asked if I used to live there.

I didn't know anyone at the orphanage; I was all alone. It was there that I learned to hate cream of wheat. Every morning we were served a lump of it with a piece of bread. While we ate, a boy would yell the number one, then another yelled two and another yelled three and so on. I remember wondering what it meant when I first arrived. What would happen was whoever was number one could scoop another serving out of the large pot, but he had to leave some for number two. The next boy would do the same, until all the cream of wheat was gone. Despite my hunger, I never participated because I hated the stuff so much.

Six months after my arrival at the orphanage, my mother, who had found work at a bakery, was stricken with pneumonia and at the age of 39 she died. The saddest part, for me, is that she died without any of her children around. She was only able to visit me in the orphanage once. It was 30 miles from Vienna which made it nearly impossible for her to come (she was living with friends after the death of my father). When I returned to Vienna years later, after the war, I remember thinking maybe it was better that my parents passed away before things got really bad. At least they had proper burials and grave sites, rather than what was to become of the people who were later rounded up by the Nazis and died horrible deaths.

Baden was a beautiful resort town, but there were not many Jews living there. We attended a regular school during the day and were supplemented with a Hebrew education at the orphanage. When I turned 13 I was given a small Bar Mitzvah; like the other boys, I received a fountain pen as a gift. I was quite popular at school because I was still a good soccer player. I wasn't teased as much, and still did well academically. I didn't know it at the time, but things were about to take a turn for the worse as the Nazis officially entered Austria in March 1938.

CHAPTER TWO

Rising Tensions

Massive celebrations were held when the Nazis arrived in Vienna. As Jews, we dreaded being anywhere near them. Anecdotally, I would say about 90 percent of non-Jews welcomed them at the time. It was announced that all Jewish schools and organizations, including orphanages, were to be closed within three months and all Jewish teachers were to leave their posts. Anti-Semitic sentiment grew even stronger following the announcement. Anything the Nazis said was taken at face value by the general public—the message being broadcast was that all of the evils in the world came from the Jews.

I remember being called into the Vice Principal's office one day. He informed me that it was to be my last day of school. He told me, "I know you are an excellent student in all subjects, but because you are a Jew I can only give you an 'A' in music." He said I was a great student and soccer player, and I would surely survive—his advice to me was to leave Austria as soon as possible. Although it was only a few weeks away, he told me I could not graduate. I told him that I had no money and asked him, "Where will I go?" He gave me a chocolate bar and wished me well. I was barely 14 years old. I could no longer attend school or live at the orphanage.

A referendum was held in April 1938 regarding the reunification of Austria with Germany. Cardinal Innitzer of the Catholic Church encouraged everyone to vote for Hitler. I remember seeing a picture of the Cardinal placing his ballot in the box. Hitler made many promises to the Catholic Church, which were never honoured. He saw himself as a god.

Tension was growing palpably in Vienna as the year 1938 progressed. One night I was walking home when I came across a little blonde girl that I recognized, weeping in the street. She said she was lost and didn't know where her mother was, or where she lived. I told her I knew where she lived and started to lead her home. On our way we were intercepted by some Hitler Youth. They taunted us, calling us dirty little Jews, and started to pull her hair while hitting us. I tried to explain to them that the girl wasn't even Jewish, but they persisted. A woman heard the commotion and came out of her home, calling the bullies dirty cowards for picking on children and hitting them with her broom until they scattered. I proceeded to bring the little girl to her mother, who was very thankful. I wanted to thank the lady who had come to our rescue, so the next day I made my way back to her apartment. The place was in shambles and no one was there. The neighbours told me that the night before, two large Schutzstaffel (SS) officers came by and beat the woman and her husband bloody. They burned the home and dragged the couple away.

My brother Leo, then almost 16 years old, was attending a Yeshiva (religious Jewish boarding school) at the time. He, along with all the other students, teachers and rabbis, was sent to a concentration camp. One day, an SS officer came to Leo, threw his dirty boots at him and said "Hey little Jew, clean and polish my boots." Leo did such a good job that he became the officer's personal attendant, cleaning his boots and performing other duties. After about three months the officer came to my brother and told him he was being promoted in the SS and returning to Berlin. The officer wrote a letter indicating that he had investigated Leo and found him not to be an "enemy of the state," and that it would be appreciated if anyone who came into contact with Leo would treat him well. He told Leo to always carry the letter with him, because he would never know when he might need it. He set Leo free from the camp so he could return to Vienna.

Kristallnacht, the infamous Night of Broken Glass, was soon to follow. What had led up to the horror of that night? Strong, undeniable evidence of hatred against Jews caused anguish throughout the Jewish and inter-married Jewish-Christian community. Some Jewish soldiers had been considered "true Germans" fighting for the Fatherland in World War I, and had even been awarded the highest German recognition (the Iron Cross). But those with foresight who lived on a tightrope in the overwhelmingly Christian community with its hatred of Judaism, understood the threatening menace.

Hitler, born in Austria, made clear in his book *Mein Kampf* his determination to unite the German community and rid Germany of all Jews.

In Vienna, violence against Jews and other "outsiders" became more acceptable to the general population. Targets were sought to blame for the German losses of World War I, and the ensuing worldwide depression of the 1930s. In anger and frustration, people took vengeance on many innocents suffering the same poverty and hunger, and gangs of bullies roamed the streets of Vienna seeking the vulnerable.

On a personal level, I feared any crowds congregating in the city. But, in search of food, I often ventured out from the apartment where I rented a small room from our family friend who had housed my mother in her final days. Her husband was a cantor so he had been sent to a concentration camp, leaving her with very few resources. I made sure to dodge any oncoming groups of thugs, sheltering in darkened alleyways until I made it back.

Eventually Leo and I were reunited in Vienna and he joined me in the small apartment. We were able to earn a bit of money because at the time if you were a Jew and had made any money (or had an income), you had to line up to get a tax receipt before you could leave the country. These lines would sometimes take days to move. At night, Leo and I would take people's places in line and when they returned in the morning they paid us for holding their spots. This way, we were able to bring a bit of money home to our mother's dear friend who housed us.

Leo and I knew we had to leave Vienna, but first we had to figure out how to ensure the safety of our sisters Josephine, Erna and Berta. There were families in Belgium and Holland that were willing to adopt them, but our priority was to keep them all together in the safest place possible. Leo felt that Paris was the answer, and we were able to locate an orphanage there that was willing to take the three of them (the Rothschild orphanage). At the age of sixteen he signed the papers as their guardian and off they went, content to be together. At that time there were still some organizations (similar to the United Jewish Appeal that exists today) that helped pay for their passage. We were sad to part ways, but we did so hoping it was the best thing for them. One of the last things Leo said to me before he died was that in view of what later happened, he regretted sending my sisters to Paris. He lived with that guilt his entire life.

On the night of November 9, 1938, the Nazis smashed windows of Jewish-owned shops and burned all but one synagogue, while the people of Vienna cheered them on. This was Kristallnacht, the Night of Broken Glass. Days before, a Jewish youth, Herschel Grynszpan, in frustration over stringent edicts against Jews, shot and killed Ernst vom Rath, the third secretary of the German Embassy in Paris. This served as the pretext for the pogrom against Jews in Nazi Germany. I witnessed Jews committing suicide by jumping out of their apartment windows. I saw a doctor I knew beaten and spit upon by people who had been his patients. I couldn't believe it; this man treated people and their children, often seeing people at night and making house calls. The people turned on him in an instant as part of the mob mentality that swept the city. Leo and I were living next to a Polish grocery store that was run by a Jewish man. Just days before, a woman came to the store without a penny to her name, looking for food. The owner gave her food and milk, and told her she could pay when she was able. I saw this woman in a group of people spitting at him that night. Only one synagogue was not destroyed, and it was because it was situated next to a Nazi office and they didn't want to risk the fire spreading to it.

Leo and I had been out walking, and as the mob grew scarier we ran back to our apartment. The owner was nowhere to be found. For our protection, we quickly locked all the doors and eliminated any lights. Hiding under the bed, we covered our ears as we shook with fear, hearing the piercing screams of our neighbours. Etched in my memory are the sounds of smashing of glass, disintegrating furniture being thrown outside, and innocents being cruelly beaten. The acrid smell of smoke was overwhelming. In my mind I can still hear the sound of boots approaching us as we hid. A couple of SS officers stormed into our place and found us. They threw us out into the street where we faced the unbelievable sights I described above, among a crowd of Jewish families. The SS officers used whips to herd us down the street towards a large meeting hall, while our non-Jewish neighbours hurled insults and spat on us. Even though anti-Jewish tensions had been steadily rising, we were still shocked by what was going on and paralyzed by fear.

Everyone was forced into a long line inside the hall, with many sobbing and trembling. We had to come before two SS officers, who demanded our names and religions then directed us to another large line of people to the left. At this moment, Leo produced the letter he had from the German officer he had served at the concentration camp. "Where are your parents?" they demanded. "They are both dead," Leo stuttered. One SS officer recognized the name of the official who had signed the letter, and he re-directed us to a much smaller line on the right where there were only two others. This small group was allowed to leave, and as we made our exit Leo uttered "Gruss Gott," which in Austrian meant "G–d be with you." The Nazi replied, "There is no G–d in Vienna, Hitler is our god." We learned the next day that the people in the large line to the left were transported to the Polish border and sent to concentration camps. Leo's letter had saved us from certain death.

When we had made our way home, a lady from across the street flagged us down—she had a letter for us. It said that we were to report to the train station at 8 a.m. the next morning and take the Kindertransport to England. If she had not spotted us that night, we would have never known and likely never escaped from Vienna with our freedom. The letter said we were allowed one suitcase for clothing and no jewelry, money, or anything else of value. The Kindertransport was initiated and sponsored by the Quakers, a Christian religious group that believed in freedom of religion. Their efforts in Britain, along with Rabbi Schonfeld and supported by Winston Churchill, prevailed upon Parliament to allow the safe entry of 10,000 unaccompanied Jewish children to be housed with British families (if they would agree to take them). Many Quaker women accompanied these children along the journey, to comfort them as they left the only family they knew, wondering what misdeeds they themselves had committed that forced them from their loved ones. Plaintive cries of "Mommy, Mommy, don't give me away! I promise to be good!" from these bewildered little ones filled the air.

As we made our way to the station the day after Kristallnacht there was so much damage, and the Jewish shop owners that remained were ordered to clean everything up. The city fined them for the damages, and if they had insurance the payouts were taken under the auspices of paying for the cost of the destruction they had suffered. We saw other Jews being forced by SS officers to clean the cobblestone streets after the terror that had occurred the night before. The station was full of children, some with their parents sending them off. Everyone was crying. I remember one child on the train, probably about seven years old, whimpering that she did not want to leave her mother. Her mother took her off the train, but her father made her get back on. He promised her they would follow her in two weeks, and that her aunt was waiting for her. I would guess that for at least 75 percent of the children on that train, it was the last time they ever saw their parents.

Shortly after departing, the train was halted and some SS officers came aboard. They inspected all of the suitcases, confiscating money and anything else that looked valuable. Leo and I didn't have much, but an officer found my stamp collection and told me "a Jewish orphan does not need a stamp album—my son will be glad to have it." The album, which had been my introduction to history, geography, stories about world leaders and events, and an appreciation for artwork and portraiture of many famous people, was lost to me forever. To this day, I have never forgiven that Nazi guard.

The train eventually crossed the border into Holland and we were met by some lovely Quaker ladies who gave us lemonade and cookies before we continued on to England. We arrived at our final destination by ship on December 31, 1938, and were taken to the Schonfeld School in London. There were tables covered in food, and the first thing I ate was cornflakes with real cream and sugar. It was such a treat for us, I must have devoured four bowls. I remember thinking it was a good thing they had a lot of toilets, because they would certainly be used. Leo, my sisters and I had escaped Vienna by the skin of our teeth, but the memories of our time there and the souls who were less fortunate than us will stay with me forever.

CHAPTER THREE

A New Start

When I left Vienna on the Kindertransport with my brother Leo in December 1938, I was 14 years old and he was 16. We hoped for a brighter future, but uncertainty prevailed. My younger sisters Josephine, Erna and Berta were promised safety in the Rothschild orphanage in Paris. Leo, as their protector, gave permission for them to go there as long as they could stay together, and they left for what was considered to be the "safest place in the world" at that time.

I was fortunate to have studied some English at school in Austria, so I was able to get through my first few days in England. The Schonfeld School had volunteers who would come and help place the children in new homes in London, and some of these volunteers took on children themselves. One volunteer in particular, Jessie Webber, was proud to have placed many children who came through the school. Her family was Jewish working class, so she never thought to adopt a child until one day her son Laurie asked her if she would consider it. Mrs. Webber noticed me when I arrived, and thinking I would be a wonderful companion to their only child, asked me if I would like to come live with them. Of course, I accepted.

The Webbers welcomed me. They were relieved to see that I carried a large blue suitcase and hoped I had sufficient clothing for a season, as they could afford very little and their son Laurie was quite tall. His clothing would have been much too large for my thin and malnourished frame. Unfortunately all I carried was an extra pair of underwear and my shirt. My beloved and only "extra" articles had been my cherished album (which had been confiscated) with many stamps that today would be quite valuable, and my small blue Bible, which is still in the possession of the Maxwell family.

The Webbers were wonderful people who treated me as their own blood. They loved art, music and literature, and to a large extent they helped restore my broken faith in humanity after everything I had witnessed back in Vienna. Laurie was about a year older than me and we became very close friends. I have a letter Laurie wrote to me, where he said he was so happy his family had taken me in because he had always wanted a brother.

While I began to settle into my new home, Laurie shared his bed and room with me until the family could afford to buy an extra bed. The Webbers had a full social life which I gladly fit into. They insisted I speak only English, not Yiddish. To encourage me, they gave me my first English novel by Charles Dickens, *Oliver Twist*. I immediately identified with the young orphaned hero and after mastering that book, I continued with many more English novels, as well as Shakespeare.

At the school where Laurie attended the last grade of elementary school, Place de Broadway in London, I was eager but concerned about my new situation. The principal announced my arrival with such a welcoming word that I felt immediately relieved. He said, "Today we have a young Jewish refugee joining us at school. He has had enough trouble in his life, so please be kind and helpful to him in any way. You'll be happy to hear he is an excellent soccer player, and he wants to play soccer for the school." Everyone cheered and I felt at home. I don't recall experiencing any anti-Semitism at all while I lived there. I resumed playing soccer and again became a top student. I was popular with my classmates and although we didn't have much at home, I was as happy as I could have been.

One of the teachers (Fritz) was also a refugee from Czechoslovakia; he had been a university professor in Prague. He often accompanied me home to help me with my English. His ulterior motive was to court the sister of Jessie Webber, a single and beautiful young lady (Esther Webber) who was often visiting her sister's home. Esther sang and another sister, Betty, played the piano for the family's entertainment. Fritz and Esther married after the war and raised a family in England.

We received frequent reports about what was happening with the Nazis to the east. In the years following the war we met many more people who had fled, including a Jewish man who lived in our condo building in Toronto. His father was an educated parliamentarian in Austria (his last name was Plashkes), and apparently his family was directly assisted in their escape by Winston Churchill.

While I was adjusting to my new life in England, the dangers from Germany brought Britain closer to involvement. Attempts at appeasement failed not long after Prime Minister Chamberlain returned from meetings with Hitler about the fate of Czechoslovakia with a paper that supposedly assured "peace in our time." This acquiescence to Hitler's demands was not only a total failure, but an encouragement to Germany to continue its aggressive actions against all its neighbours, including Poland, which it invaded in September 1939. Not long after, Britain was officially at war with Nazi Germany and we knew we were in for a long and difficult siege. Our new Prime Minister, Winston Churchill, gave constant encouragement to the valiant British people in their struggle against the Nazis after the fall of France. His speeches were the guiding force through many setbacks and losses until total victory was finally declared in 1945.

Leo and I had once again been separated, but we stayed in close contact. He lived with a family in Wales and studied mechanics, while making regular visits to see me in London. In Wales, he walked by an elderly woman's home each day and would often help her around the house or run errands for her. Leo was eventually approved for a visa to move to the United States where he intended to live in Detroit with friends of our father, the Freunds. Leo's approval was contingent upon the fact that he had been born in Poland; there was a somewhat limited acceptance of Polish-born immigrants into the U.S. at that time. Thankfully, Mr. and Mrs. Freund were his guarantors—everyone coming to America at that time had to have a guarantor to ensure they would not be a burden on the government. When Leo went to say goodbye to the elderly woman, she gave him a letter to deliver to her son, Mr. Matthew Smith, who was the head of the union at the Ford car plant. The letter introduced Leo to her son and requested that he find a job for him, if possible.

After arriving in Detroit, and staying with the Freund family for a few days, Leo acted on his initiative and made an appointment to meet Matthew Smith. As it was still the Great Depression, there were thousands looking for work in Detroit but thanks to his connection, Leo was quickly given a job working on the assembly line at the Ford Motor Company. The salary was abundant enough for him to live decently, and to help the wonderful Freund family financially as well. After the war, Leo studied while working to become a real estate appraiser, acknowledged and certified to be an advisor on property for the state of Michigan.

I was in London during the air raids and it was terrifying! The German bombers were intent on terrorizing and demoralizing the British people. Each night they deliberately bombed residential targets, killing people, destroying homes, churches, hospitals and schools. The Britons spent nights by darkening their homes, hiding in dug-out bomb shelters and tunnels in the London Underground while keeping their hopes up by singing in spite of it all. The buildings around them shook convulsively through the night; the sounds and screeches of falling bombs never let up until dawn when the brave souls could finally leave their cells to assess the damage. Each day they worked to clear the remnants of the night before, as they bravely attempted to work and reassigned housing to the now-homeless. The voices of Churchill and members of the Royal Family continued to boost their morale as things became more desperate for them all.

I continued with school until 1940 when the Webbers moved to Manchester, where Mr. Webber opened a small shop making and repairing cabinets. I was sixteen and a half, so I continued with school in Manchester for a time, but soon dropped out so I could work full-time. Mr. Webber connected me with a company where I met others who had escaped their home countries via the Kindertransport. As the war heated up, these boys were interned as enemy aliens, sometimes along with captured Nazis. To this day I still have no idea why, but for some reason I was not selected. I did have some restrictions, though, because I came from Austria. I could not own a radio, and I had to get a permit to ride a bicycle to get to work (and to school prior to getting my job).

One of my first encounters with official rules, which I learned to follow with strict obedience, was my attempt to join the British Armed Forces. As Britain entered the war against the Nazi scourge, Churchill's dominant and forceful words gave courage to the Brits who rose every morning after nights of bombing on civilian targets. With food rationed, goods scarce, and husbands and sons in harm's way, the British people found the inner strength to keep going and to overcome.

My brother Laurie enlisted as soon as he was age-eligible and served in the jungles of Burma throughout most of the war years. Thankfully he survived to return to England and marry a wonderful young lady, Frieda Isaacson, who had a large family of her own. Love and encouragement came from my new friends and they all welcomed me into their circles.

I went with him to the recruiting centre and tried to enlist but I was too young and small (at the time I weighed only 119 pounds).

The recruiting officer told me I should go back to kindergarten. I left in embarrassment but returned when I was a day over seventeen and a half, with Mrs. Webber's written permission. The same recruiting officer who had rejected me before recognized me. "What kept you?" he asked. "I was expecting you yesterday."

Before my induction into the army, those of us who escaped from Germany, Austria and Czechoslovakia were classified as "enemy aliens." Some of the older ones were interned on the Isle of Man or sent to Canada and Australia. We were not allowed to join the regular army, only the Pioneer Corps—to repair streets, bridges and tunnels, due to the majority of the male population assigned to martial duties.

As a young, enthusiastic recruit, I first had to pass my medical exam and then report to the Army Centre Hayton in Liverpool. My adoptive mother, Mrs. Webber, accompanied me to the train, kissed me goodbye and gave me ten shillings. At my destination I was told to eat lunch, shown my sleeping quarters, and informed that I would get my uniform the next day. At lunch, another recruit, a strong fellow about six-foot-two exchanged a few words of greeting and asked me, "Hey kid, do you have any money?" I should have been suspicious but wanted to have a friend in the rough area of Liverpool. I responded that I did indeed have ten shillings. He suggested that we go out and see the town together that evening.

A few hours later he brought me a uniform that was really too big but he told me, "This will have to do!" Furthermore, he led me not through the front entrance but around the back way, hopefully unnoticed. We walked towards a pub called the Bucket of Blood. My instincts should have warned me about taking this venture, but not wanting to be a "sissy" I naively entered a noisy, raucous, and boisterous drinking establishment. He asked me, "What are you drinking, lad?" I responded with my current favourite, lemonade, at which he balked and goaded me with "You're a soldier now, you must drink what I order!"

That was a large mug of warm English beer, and he joined me. Another drink followed, and I became slightly tipsy. He took my money to pay for the drinks then took me aside, confiding in me that he would now "fix me up."

I had no idea what he meant, as he introduced me to a brazen woman of about 30 wearing dark red lipstick smeared across her mouth. "Come here honey, I'll look after you," she said, and led me out of the pub. At this point, the military police with their red hats appeared to contain the mob, and they yelled at me: "Soldier, put on your cap, button up your coat!" She loudly blasted them with some choice words, which I, in my drunken condition, repeated.

The next thing I knew they threw me in a military truck and took me to the jail where they undressed me, doused me in a cold shower, put my clothes back on, and put me to bed with a blanket. Three other derelicts shared this cell with me. In the morning I was handed a razor, shaving cream, and a much better-fitting uniform. I faced a stern Major and other officers. The charges against me were read:

(1) Leaving the camp without permission,
(2) Being drunk and disorderly,
(3) Threatening the military police officers in their duty, and
(4) Being a "disgrace" to the army.

The Major turned to the Sergeant-Major and asked, "How long has this man been in the army?" The response was, "Sir, he came yesterday!" Next they asked who was with me, but I kept a tight lip and said that I was alone.

The Major determinedly stated, "I will teach you a lesson. Every day after your duty, at 16:00, you will peel potatoes until 20:00!"

This was very exhausting after the all-day rigors of exercising and marching. After three days, the sports officer of my regiment came to the kitchen where I worked and commented, "Soldier, I noticed on your application that you played soccer for your school. How would you like to play for the army?"

I said, "How can I? I have to peel potatoes as a punishment."

"Leave it to me," he confided. "I'll look after it."

I became very popular at the regiment because I never divulged the name of the person who led me astray. I became a valued member of the soccer team as well, but the misdemeanors were marked on my records. Eventually, they were expunged. One day, I went to my commanding officer and told him I didn't join the army to build bridges—I joined to fight. He had me transferred to the Tank Corps.

From 1942 to 1944 I was stationed at Aldershot, where we trained every day. This generally consisted of a ten-mile march with full equipment. It was tough but we were young, so after a hard day we would return to the barracks to wash up, then go into town for the dances. I became close friends with Evan Williams, a young man from Wales. He would come with me to synagogue and happily wore a yarmulke there, and I joined him at church as well. I remember he asked me why Jews don't go to confession every day. I told him that we save up all year for one holy day of confession, Yom Kippur.

We didn't know anything about the concentration camps at that time—almost no one did. I do believe that Churchill and Roosevelt knew, because I heard later that a Jew had escaped from one of the camps and lived to tell his tale. We followed the war by radio, and were encouraged when the Nazis surrendered at Stalingrad. For us, it showed that the Nazis were not invincible and could, in fact, be defeated.

There was a call put out for glider pilots, so Evan and I both signed up. Out of 400 people, only 40 passed the training, including Evan and myself. Part of our rigorous mental and physical training was, of course, learning the physics of flying, actually being in the cockpit, and eventually piloting a glider. The prospect of being "on air" was at first a terrifying thought, but I considered it to be an exciting adventure. I was determined to do my part in overcoming the scourge of Nazi Germany.

First, we had to pass a flight test to see if we could tolerate the gravitational forces required. We were ordered to put on the special gear provided and arrive at an open field where instructors awaited us. The "Tiger Moth" plane that we approached had an open cockpit and two seats—the front for the pilot, with his controls on the dashboard in front of him. The tall, older Lieutenant assigned to me asked, "Hey kid, have you ever flown before?" Of course, none of the recruits had, as yet. "Okay, here's your opportunity! Climb up the step and into the seat. Make sure your seatbelt is affixed and your two shoulder straps are secure."

When ready, he revved the engine; the propeller began its whirring, and we raced down the runway eventually rising above the ground. It was exhilarating! At approximately 2,000 feet up, he began some maneuvers. Left, right, circling and even upside-down! I hung firmly to the two straps. Eventually he levelled off and gradually lowered the plane until it touched down.

"May I ask you a personal question?" he queried.

"Of course" I answered directly, without hesitation.

"How is your underwear?"

"Sir, I believe it's still perfectly dry!"

"You'll make a good pilot then."

Our next challenge was to learn how to efficiently fly and steer a glider. The first planes we were assigned to were small versions of the ones we would eventually fly in our missions. They held two pilot seats at the front facing the instrument panel. It took me about eight hours to master the controls, eventually fly solo, and learn about the heavy fortified rope that towed us behind a Lancaster bomber. This rope was to be released from the larger plane by being cut off when we, the pilots, judged that we were approaching our target. We would land in the best terrain possible nearby, knowing there was no retreat for us. Our engineless gliders were silent, so we could land without the enemy hearing our approach and landing.

We soon felt confident about our abilities and were invited to observe an exhibition of gliders at a location near Aldershot. During the exhibition, one of the demonstrating gliders unfortunately crashed, killing one young recruit pilot. However, we remained unnerved, still confident we could fulfill our duty.

Before our official transfer, I went to meet Evan's family in Wales. They were lovely people; Evan came from generations of coal miners. His grandfather told me Evan would be the first in his family to attend university after the war, and that he would become a medical doctor. They promised to do whatever they could for me as well. When we left, Evan's mother kissed us both and made us promise to look after each other.

Our pay at that time was two shillings a day. We didn't need much since our food was provided already, just boot polish and cigarettes (which at the time cost only two pence for a pack). A drink at a bar would cost 20 or 30 pence. The initial training was arduous, consisting of marching, hurling bayonets, running with full packs and climbing uneven rockery and hills. We deserved the few days' leave before our initial proposed action. On December 31, 1943, another glider pilot, Fred, and I were on a short leave in London. We were at a pub having a choice beer, when four beautiful and well-dressed models entered and approached us. To our great surprise, they invited us to join them as their guests for a dinner hosted by their employer D.H. Evans, a famous fashion designer in London.

We quickly and eagerly agreed, and joined them in their cars to drive to a large banquet hall where mostly young women and servicemen were celebrating, dancing and singing. We toasted and drank until almost midnight, when I noticed Fred had passed out drinking the sparkling champagne. I was next, due to my inexperience with drinking liquor, and did not really know what had happened until the next morning. Fred and I woke up each in a luxurious bed, in beautiful pajamas, our uniforms beautifully pressed and folded nearby. A sign on the wall said: "If you need assistance, pull the cord for the butler."

At our request the butler appeared and explained that when we both passed out, Mr. Evans had him undress us and put us to bed. We then showered, shaved and dressed and the butler handed us each an envelope with a note stating Mr. Evans' thanks for our service, and gifting us with 50 pounds each! Considering our salaries of two shillings a day, 50 pounds was an incredible amount of money. What a great surprise and a wonderful show of appreciation. I'll never forget his generosity!

Fred and I returned to our base, where our trainer was a burly Sergeant Major with a large moustache. He told us we knew nothing, but when we completed our training he would have to show us respect by saluting us. Our training was grueling but we made it through, and both received promotions to the rank of Sergeant (along with a raise in pay to 12 shillings a day).

As history will tell you, D-Day was quickly approaching. Evan and I were in the Army Air Corps, 6th Airborne. We had been confined to camp near the south coast since May 30, 1944—no outgoing mail, no outgoing or incoming calls. We had been constantly training—flying, loading, and unloading planes. We were trained to do our best! There was no time to feel fear or worry about danger.

On the morning of June 5, 1944, we were ordered to assemble at the Sergeants' Mess to be addressed by Lieutenant-General Browning (he was the oldest, married to Daphne du Maurier). He said he didn't have to remind us of the air raids on London. "You boys will be the first ones in, and many of you won't come back," he warned. He advised us to write letters to whomever we wanted, which would be mailed if we did not return. The room went silent as the gravity of the situation sank in and we each held our private thoughts; we were all thinking of our families, significant others and close friends. I wrote to the Webbers, thanking them for adopting me. I also wrote to my brothers, Leo and Laurie.

My letters reached Laurie in the jungles of Burma, and Leo who had joined the American Army Air Force as a bombardier whose plane was hit in the fields of Romania. He and his two other Irish crew members were able to bail out and were rescued by guerrilla fighters under Marshal Tito. His experience allowed him to take part with others in 1948 to help create the Israeli Air Force. I also wrote, not knowing about their situation, to my three sisters, who had been sent to the Rothschild orphanage in Paris. They were rounded up during the Nazi occupation; I hoped they would receive my personal letter and it would give them strength to stay alive.

I also had to attend a meeting that consisted mainly of Jewish pilots. We were told that there had been reports of Nazis torturing and killing soldiers they captured who had Jewish-sounding names. "You gentlemen may well likely be in much more grave danger if you are captured by the Nazis. Your Jewish names will mark you for harsh treatment, deportation to a concentration camp, or immediate death," the Lieutenant-General told us. We were advised to pick new, Anglicized names out of the phone book and we would be given identification with those names in case we were captured. Without hesitation, we realized the importance of his order. To save ourselves and to assist our fellow servicemen, we silently thanked our superiors for their consideration of our circumstances. I quickly turned to the local phone directory to scan the names beginning with the letters "Ma." My given name was Max Meisels, but from that day on I became Martin Maxwell, the name of another who would unknowingly contribute to my safety.

CHAPTER FOUR

Historic Missions

The invasion of Normandy was to take place on June 6, 1944, under the code name of Operation Overlord. We were an early part of the raid, under our own Operation Deadstick. Just before 11 p.m. on June 5, 1944 we took off; I was co-piloting one of six enclosed glider planes with Sergeant Cotterill. We had about 20 specially trained commandos on board, along with some Jeeps and other military equipment. We flew over the North Sea in the dark for about an hour with no escort except for the Lancaster bomber that towed us, and which left us once we had judged our landing. We cut the towing rope and hoped we would reach our destination—Pegasus Bridge.

Not all of the gliders landed well (some hit the water or the fields), but we made it in the dark without crashing, and silently. We landed 200 or 300 yards away from the bridge. Our mission was to secure two bridges so that in the morning when the invasion began, the Germans would not be able to bring in their reinforcements. We were instructed to avoid using our bullets at first by taking out the sentries with bayonets if possible, so as not to wake the sleeping garrison nearby. I did what I had to do and survived, unscathed.

We saw paratroopers landing and one of the officers told me to go see if they were ours. As the night went on, hundreds of parachutists joined us until we were fully relieved two days later, after confirming that the bridge was completely held by our Allied forces. Exhausted and spent, we rejoiced at our success. We were ready to go home.

Returning via the beach to reach the submarine which would transport us, we surveyed the destruction and many of our human losses with great sorrow. Many of our young lads still lay amidst the carnage. I remember one young man, red-haired and maybe 17 or 18 years old, his helmet askew and bullet-ridden head and body shifting helplessly as the shore waves swept over him. My deepest sorrow and sense of loss exist even to this day when the world recalls the horrendous losses of D-Day and the fortitude necessary to overcome evil. I remember thinking, "Will anybody remember you in the years to come, that you gave your young life so that we could live in freedom? For our tomorrows you bravely gave your short life here and now."

My evacuation by submarine included only four other pilots. My first inclination was to declare the submarine's immersion beneath the water and ability to be seen by the enemy ships to be extremely dangerous, and we hesitated somewhat. However, these brave British seamen forcefully declared that we were even crazier to go up in a plane made of plywood, canvas and tar, with no engine or power to escape and only one way to go—down. It never occurred to me at the time how risky it was. We were given "escape money," to bribe enemy officers in case we were captured. A couple days before we left, we were gambling and I lost a lot of money. Just before we left, the officer came to me and gave me all my money back.

From the submarine we were delivered by truck to a tiny village on England's shore to a great welcome, as we were needed again to continue the fight. Britain was short of glider pilots required for further invasions into Europe. We reached the Cambrian Hills with the remaining rescued pilots and gratefully relaxed on leave for approximately two weeks; then to return for the next major assault.

I never took any joy in the killing that inevitably comes when you participate in a war, but given the prejudice I experienced as a boy and horrible acts perpetrated by the Nazis that I witnessed over the course of my life up to that point, I do not feel any remorse. D-Day was the beginning of the end of World War II and I am proud of how I performed the small role that I had in it.

After our return to England and our leave, we came back to our training camp to prepare for the next operation. While we waited, listening to the radio, we captured the voice of a German reporter named "Sagittarius" stating that there was an imminent invasion of Holland.

General Montgomery had his own plans to land forces behind the German lines. Several bridges had to be taken, including the farthest one over the River Rhine. This was the bridge at Arnhem. A victory would ensure a quick invasion of Germany in 1944. This would be labelled "Operation Market Garden."

This was an extremely dangerous mission, as just a few weeks earlier a young reconnaissance mission pilot was shocked to find a large German tank division stationed just a few miles outside Arnhem. He sensed the danger and immediately reported to General Montgomery the folly in subjecting British troops to such extreme difficulty. "They would be cut to pieces!"

General Montgomery took no heed of this warning and he immediately ordered the officer home on "sick leave," telling him he had not been feeling well and needed a rest! With the officer out of the way, Montgomery proceeded by calling a meeting with Lieutenant-General Browning.

Browning asked, "How long will it take our tanks to reach Nijmegen (the second bridge once conquered) to relieve us at Arnhem?" Montgomery answered, "Two days." Browning responded, "Sir, we can only hold out for three days maximum, in case of delay. Perhaps this is a bridge too far."

Nevertheless, on September 17, 1944, we prepared ourselves for the assault called Operation Market Garden. We left at mid-morning on that date, six gliders, headed for outside Arnhem after surveying maps, details and conditions. The weather was cold but clear, as we left carrying mostly high-ranking Polish officers because this group had now joined our fight. They carried rifles and machine guns. Our gliders were the same type as the ones we used on D-Day. We wore goggles and gloves and carried other essential equipment, and were motivated by our earlier success in France.

After a very smooth flight, we landed exactly at our target in daylight to a welcome by huge throngs of the Dutch people (men, women, the elderly and children). The sky filled with more and more gliders that followed us and landed in the same area. Cheering, waving and chanting continued at our arrival. A young girl of approximately ten years greeted us with the English question, "Chewing gum?" which we had thoughtfully carried to distribute and cheer the people who had been so forcefully subjugated and were looking forward to these little treats. Also, a middle-aged man in worn clothes came forward and hugged us as he pulled out of his jacket a special bottle of liquor which he said he had kept safely for our hoped-for arrival! We heartily toasted with him and quickly prayed for the Dutch people and the rest of Europe.

Then our troop had a small meal from the cases in our gliders and were instructed by our commander, Sergeant-Major Lord, to start to dig ditches for our own protection in case we were attacked. The town of Oosterbeek would be our area. It was on the outskirts of Arnhem. We were advised that we had sufficient water and food to last three days, and not any longer. Therefore it was necessary to ration all these fundamentals. The expectation was that our tanks from Nijmegen would reach us and link up and relieve us in two to three days.

Exhausted after the flight, and the hard work of ditch-digging, we were allowed to sleep in the trenches but eight-hour shifts were required to keep watch. Pillows and blankets that traveled with us on our gliders were distributed.

To our dismay and shock, we awoke suddenly to gunfire the next morning, seeing more gliders on the ground being shot down and destroyed, and many parachutists from Lancasters or Sterlings being immobilized. It was a demoralizing and horrendous sight as we realized that the Germans were prepared for us, and we no longer had the three or four days we hoped for. From our location toward the bridge, we had to maintain our section to protect our troops who were moving up.

German tanks constantly bombarded us; some of us in trucks, others on patrol. Each bombardment injured and killed many of us. Our situation was very difficult, but we held on!

Aiding us in the midst of this horror were the attendants of the Red Cross. These were young and handy volunteers who joined us as "conscientious objectors," and who demonstrated great bravery in tending to the wounded and administering morphine to those in great pain while in the midst of a debilitating battle. Later, a station was erected for the wounded who had to be carried to a safer location. Each day our casualties mounted. Food and medicine were in short supply and for those of us still active, we knew that our rescuers would not be coming any time soon.

Several attempts by the brave Dutch civilians were made to give us food, water and some help. But they and even their young children were killed by the Germans if caught. As this bombardment continued, our numbers were depleted and in this pitiful way, our rations became sufficient for the remaining few of us.

Our air force also tried to get supplies to us; however, persistently cloudy skies prevented them from reaching their targets and most of it fell into jubilant German hands. Our casualties mounted; Red Cross volunteers continued to carry away the dead and injured to bring them to a clearly marked house that had been converted into a makeshift hospital.

Meanwhile, the bad news was that our own forces, whose job it was to capture the bridge over the Rhine, had managed to reach only the lower part of the bridge. They, too, suffered tremendous casualties.

After seven days our commanding officer gave me an order. "Maxwell, you seem to be the ablest one still here. Make your way carefully to the Hotel Hartenstein."* The building was visible from where we waited. In the midst of the clamour, gunfire and bombing, he reminded me to tell our officers, who were barely able to maintain themselves, that we in the trenches had no water, supplies or medicine left. "Sergeant Maxwell, find out what is happening, and come back and report to us what we should do!" he desperately cried out to me.

I climbed out and traversed about 15 yards when a huge tank bombardment hit the trench area all of us were in! This blow forced me to turn around, slamming me against a tree and tearing off the whole top of my uniform. The shredded remains of my uniform, when later discovered, carried my name, rank and identification. Normally a uniform in this condition, when mailed to my British family, would mean "Missing in Action: Presumed Killed."

Screaming in pain, I could see that my right hand was broken and my thigh was smashed, sticking out through my shirt. I fell into unconsciousness.

Unaware of the time lapse, I came to; I heard two men with sticks probing the trenches. "It looks like this one is still alive!" They proceeded to give me strong pills and water to drink. They bandaged my right hand and tied splints to my right leg before they half-carried, half-dragged me to the previously mentioned Red Cross hospital building.

* The hotel has since been converted into a military museum honouring the British and others who fought there.

In my painful state, I was overcome by the sights and sounds of moaning injured as well as those silenced by death. As I passed so many, another weakened soldier reached out to me and handed me a picture of his family. He grabbed me and told me to tell them, "I have just received my Last Rites, and I am thinking of them and love them. I hope you will survive to do this for me." I was told later that he died shortly after.

The Red Cross workers placed me down gently on a pillow on the ground. Next to me, another injured soldier whose left foot had been partially severed urged me, "Kid, don't go to sleep! If you do, you may never wake up!"

As I began to revive and came to my senses, I answered him, "If we stay here, we'll all die. Why don't you and I take a chance and crawl to the German lines? If we surrender, maybe we can be helped at a better place if there is a hospital there!" It was a torturous crawl for us, but we made it to the German lines and approached them. They helped us onto a German truck to take us to Wilhelmina Hospital. From the truck, as we went through Arnhem, the most horrible sights met our eyes. At least two dozen Dutch men, women and children were hanging by their necks, turning black, and wearing signs in German—"Traitors and collaborators, this is what happens to you."

In addition, the town of Arnhem was in ruins. We were later informed that a temporary armistice had been called, for approximately 36 hours, and that was why we were saved. The time was allotted for sick and wounded on both sides to get to an area of treatment.

Who were the caregivers? As most of the nurses and doctors were removed by the Nazis, we were treated by very young girls and boys who helped relieve our pain with drugs. They washed and cared for us, and provided us with meagre food (bread and some cheese). It took three days for a medic to get to us, as the most severely injured needed urgent care, such as amputations and other surgeries.

One more week slowly passed. As I became slightly stronger, approximately twenty others and I were transferred by truck to the SS barracks in Apeldoorn to be interrogated. I dreaded what might be ahead of us and silently thanked my commanding officer for having the vision to tell me and others to change our names from obvious Jewish surnames to Anglo-Saxon ones.

With some assistance, we were led to our cots in the German barracks and were allowed to sleep. In the morning, we slowly made our way to another room where a small bit of sustenance was provided for us. We tried to informally communicate with our fellow comrades, keeping the lines of support open from one to another. By about 10 a.m. each of us was taken separately to a second room and given fuller investigations. They pumped us for answers to military maneuvers, which we truthfully were unable to provide.

"Where are the Allies going next?"

"How many troops were in Nijmegen?"

"What was your eventual goal?"

My name and rank were the only answers I could give. Finally, exhausted, we were given a meagre meal and allowed to rest. After only an hour I overheard two other SS officers, frustrated at the lack of information from us, speaking in German (which I understood). "The best thing we can do now is kill all these bastards!" The second officer, who was of a higher rank (possibly an SS general), urged him, "Don't be stupid; in six months' time they will reach Berlin. If you kill them, you'll be declared a war criminal!"

I slept fitfully, despite the pain that still persisted. They told us we would be going to a prisoner of war camp, called 11B, Fallingbostel, near Hanover, Germany. For the journey, which would take only a few hours, they gave us each two pieces of bread and some cheese. On the way, however, the Air Force destroyed part of the tracks. This caused a great delay into the night as we could not proceed.

Many years later, after the war, I was speaking to a large group of Canadian, American, British and French officers and I posed this question—"How is it that you bombed the train tracks which led to the prisoner of war camp so many times, but never once did you bomb the tracks to Auschwitz?" The officers were silent, but after my speech a British and an American officer called me aside and gave me the jarring answer.

"We were specifically ordered not to do so, as both Churchill and Roosevelt, who knew about the horrors of the camps, followed their advisors who said, 'What's the point of rescuing the Jews? Where will they go? Nobody wants to take them in.'"

By noon the next day we had finally arrived at the camp, but the effort for us in our condition caused us to move at a debilitating pace to reach the gate marked 11B. They wouldn't let us in—they were planning to keep us from getting some urgent nourishment of which we were severely deprived. Adjacent to our destination was a Russian prison camp, and when the inmates noticed what was happening they selflessly threw some meagre rations of their own to reach us in our destitute state. What a sacrifice it was for them to give us some sustenance and in doing so, deprive themselves of food!

After an hour's delay, the gates were opened for us and we were finally told to go into the camp. We were led to a barracks and each assigned a bed. Exhausted and hungry we took our places, but it wasn't until 5 p.m. that we were finally given some bread. This camp was overwhelming in size and in number of prisoners. We were the newly arrived, but many prisoners had been captured in the disastrous battle at Dunkirk, and they were already so accustomed to the conditions that they were labeled "stalag-happy" because they had accepted their fate whatever it was, as any of their comrades who had tried to escape were caught and severely dealt with.

Our camp, mostly British, held only ranks of Sergeant and above. According to the Geneva Convention, officers of this rank were not forced to do any physical work for the Germans. This factor, perhaps, helped us to barely survive. Our two "meals" of the day consisted of (a) dry bread and rotten cheese bits, and (b) "ersatz" bread again and a cup of turnip soup. In these terrible conditions, and with the scarcity of bread, the worst crime one could commit was "stealing" another's bread. The offender would be thrown into the common latrine for two days. If they survived, it served as notice to everyone else never to take a morsel away from a fellow prisoner.

In the beginning each of us received a Red Cross parcel containing candies, chocolates, cookies, peanuts and a small package of cigarettes. Although at that time I was a heavy smoker, I could see the advantage of trading the cigarettes with the Nazi guards for extra pieces of bread or cake.

If anyone committed even a minor infraction, such as not keeping our places swept, we were all punished by being made to stand outside without blankets for an hour or more in freezing temperatures. It was mandatory to salute any German officer as we passed by. One brave or forgetful soldier neglected to do so, and was immediately sent to the prison jail for two weeks. After a few days, his surprising report was that being incarcerated was more pleasant than being in the barracks! The jail was heated, the food was somewhat better, and he did not have to stand "on parade" in the cold! Before long, everyone caught on to be punished by going to jail, and the building was filled to capacity until the Germans figured it out and discontinued this "punishment" in return for a harsher treatment.

After a few months, we hoped for some good news and began to hear the sound of bombers overhead. British ones, dropping their loads on the nearby city of Hanover. This gave us great elation, and raised our spirits. One of the higher ranking among us pulled me aside and said, "I know you understand German. Try to listen in and glean some information about the Allied progress. The guards must be getting nervous, maybe they'll divulge some facts!"

Each day, one of us yelled "Football Results" which gave details of our advances. A military man of our rank had a hidden radio (forbidden) and disguised the winning numbers to represent the Allied advances. I marvel, and thank my fellow prisoners, that most knew I was Jewish but never considered blowing my cover in that precarious situation in the camp.

As Christmas 1944 approached, one of our "stalag-happy" chums announced, "Cheer up boys, at Christmas time I promise you, we'll have a chicken!" Realizing the absurdity of his comment, and believing him to be nuts, we laughed it off and dreamed. Astonishingly, just as Christmas Eve approached, he cooked us a chicken on his rotating spit over the flame. He cut and distributed the most delicious and mouth-watering meal we ever had! He asked us, "Did you enjoy the chicken?" We overwhelmingly agreed that we did. "But how did you achieve this?" we asked.

"Do you remember the cat that belonged to a German officer that went missing? Well, I caught it and each day fed it bits of bread to fatten it. So in the future, when you are liberated and get asked about your best Christmas dinner, you can tell this story about the wonderful chicken you ate here!"

Cruelty had no bounds and we witnessed the most sadistic actions that man could devise. At the Russian camp adjacent to ours, one of the German guards announced that he would get himself one Russian every day. What he meant was that he would torture and kill one emaciated Russian prisoner by the vilest means available to him. He set his dogs on his prey and intentionally pursued a specific individual so that we, from our camp, would witness this horror. The dogs would mercilessly attack on command, biting limbs and not stopping until their poor victim stopped screaming and was dead.

In secret retribution, the forlorn Russian prisoners were able to take a wooden stick, shave the end to a fierce point and attack these two dogs as they ran to torment another Russian. The dogs were maimed sufficiently to prevent them from carrying on the commands of their German owner. In retaliation, the Germans took several prisoners at random and shot them dead.

CHAPTER FIVE

Liberation

As March 1945 neared its end, the Germans decided to take the nine known Jewish prisoners of war in our camp and send them away to a concentration camp. We, the other prisoners, bravely announced that we firmly objected to this order and that we would not follow other orders if they continued in this direction. Hundreds of us demonstrated! It took two days for them to reconsider, but we held our ground and they soon reversed their decision. They would be declared war criminals as this proposed action was against the Geneva Convention.

In the last few months we all suffered from starvation but the Nazis, realizing their plight, began to be less severe towards us. Still, any Red Cross parcels never reached us, because the food or medicine in them was stolen along the way. One morning in April we woke up to find three Nazi tanks facing our camp. We feared the worst—that these machines were there to annihilate us. We were determined to fight back as long as necessary to bring them down. However, our annihilation was not their intention. They wanted to march us into the nearby hills in order for them to bargain with the Allies to let the German guards advance in order to return back to their homes. In exchange we, the captured prisoners, would be able to join our allies and find refuge.

The British forces refused. Consequently, with nowhere else to go except back to the camp, the German guards all disappeared, leaving us unattended. Several days later, on May 1, 1945, we rejoiced at the sight of the first British tank that came to rescue us. We were finally liberated!

One touching moment occurred when a blinded Russian prisoner took me by the hand and asked me to do him the favour of placing his hand on top of the British tank, in order for him to believe he was finally free. "After four years, I am finally free!" he exclaimed. By the next afternoon, to help our recovery, trucks arrived with the miracle sustenance of food—eggs, soup, bread, cheese, bully beef, Spam, milk powder, and especially medicine delivered by male Red Cross nurses.

We were warned that due to the delicate conditions of our systems, we should eat slowly and introduce very little at a time. In fact, our very first nutrition was from Jell-O because it was easy on the stomach. Several did not heed this warning; one sergeant with extreme hunger swallowed eight eggs and suffered the consequences. He became very ill and succumbed, presumably from a combination of this and other illnesses contracted during his incarceration. At the time of this rescue I weighed 87 pounds but I cautiously and slowly consumed my first meal of Jell-O, one soft-boiled egg and a large piece of bread—the best meal I can remember in my lifetime.

We began to enjoy our limited freedom until we could be returned to Britain. During this time we noticed two Jeeps arriving at our camp. They were driven by high-ranking Russian officers who were there to help repatriate the Russian prisoners-of-war. They cheerfully greeted us, and motioning at my British navigation watch, indicated that they would like it.

"What can you give us in exchange?" I retorted. They offered us one of their army Jeeps and five gallons of petrol! Seeing this exchange as a means of exploring outside the camp, I gladly gave up my watch as my friend and I climbed in and left for a ride. We packed some limited supplies of ham, eggs, cheese and bread to take with us and we proceeded to drive, not knowing where we were going until we reached a crossroads. Two signs came into view. The left side indicated Bergen-Belsen, the infamous concentration camp that we had heard about, but we did not really know all of the horrible details at that time. The other sign read "Kinder Haim" (Children's Home). Following this road for about a mile and a half, we entered a barbed wire enclosure of grass and earth, and were appalled by the sight of wild dogs tearing at the bodies of dead young children. At the loud blast of our horn they scampered away. Suddenly an emaciated young girl of about six years old ran up to us, putting her arms around my friend's leg, and yelled "Papa, Papa!"

At this point, an older woman ran out of a ramshackle low-level building, arms outstretched and exhorted, "This is little Hannah, one of almost two hundred abandoned children of different nationalities or foreign backgrounds. They are mostly children of workers who abandoned them to our care during the total destruction of this area.

"Whenever Hannah sees a man in uniform, she hopes it would be her father, a Polish soldier who was killed in the war." Every crumb of food from our Jeep was handed over to this brave and compassionate lady to help her children attain some nourishment. We promised to return the next day with as much food as possible.

Despondent, on the way home in the nearby village we passed a store which had a large doll in the window. We knocked on the glass, and when the proprietor came out we showed him the only item of monetary value we had—my hidden cigarettes. He gladly accepted ten cigarettes in exchange for the beautiful doll and we told him it was for a very special and deserving homeless child.

Early the next morning, after our sumptuous breakfast, we quickly loaded the army food still on the table along with a huge roll of cheese which my friend obtained from the quartermaster in exchange for his navigation watch. Off we went, looking forward to the delivery to help the starving little ones. When we arrived at the camp, all the children were eagerly awaiting our visit, and they gleefully yelled "Tommy, Tommy" (the nickname for an English soldier).

We unloaded the food to the woman in charge of four other lady volunteers, so they could distribute it to the eager, hungry mouths. I didn't see little Hannah and I immediately asked the supervisor where she was so I could give her the special gift. She shook her head sadly, and looking down, she told us that little Hannah had died in the night. Her last words were "Papa, Papa." My friend Fred and I mournfully made our way back to the Jeep, where we both sat down and cried for little Hannah and all the other destitute and forgotten little Hannahs in the world.

On our return to the camp we were greeted by several newly-arrived British officers and we informed them of the destitute children's home. They promised us they would go there and give them as much aid as possible.

Our joyous mood of victory was tempered by our impatience to get home and be back with our loved ones. As so many had to be repatriated—servicemen and women still in the ranks, sick and wounded needing medical attention, as well as we, the prisoners of war—this was a monumental and coordinated movement, which relied on the availability of vehicles, ships and planes for transportation home.

After many days, we were given instructions to leave the camp and were repatriated to England, first by truck to the nearest train, then by ship. I could hardly wait to see my adoptive family, the wonderful Webbers in Manchester, and I rejoiced to know that they had been informed that I survived.

What an exuberant welcome! Finally on May 10, 1945, we were individually interviewed and assigned placement for return. We were each compensated financially depending upon the time of internment, as we were officially in the services during the time of our capture. Our ship landed on Britain's shore, and I was finally reunited with the Webbers in Manchester, who were overjoyed at my arrival. My adoptive brother Laurie had to endure a much longer wait to return from his service in Burma. Shortly after his return, he resigned from the Royal Air Force, planning to join his father Maurice in the family business (a small furniture manufacturing company). Although I was extremely grateful to be considered a part of it, I felt my future lay elsewhere, and continued to remain in Army service. Mr. Webber had erected a sign, "M. Webber and Sons," and was very disappointed when I thanked him but chose to stay in the Army for the time being.

After several weeks' leave during which time I enjoyed many social events—dances, visiting the Webbers' relatives, going to movies with friends and dating many beautiful young ladies—soon I was called by the British war office; I was informed that my skills in understanding German and my war experience made me suitable to be considered as one of the assistant commanders of a large German prisoner-of-war camp holding Germans of all ranks, but mostly privates, corporals and sergeants.

My job was to be the interpreter during interviews of German prisoners and try to determine their level of participation in the German hierarchy, and their degree of innocence or guilt in carrying out their orders. Many claimed to be merely low-level militants following orders, but were suspected of being higher-ranking officers who actually gave orders of a more harmful nature against prisoners and so-called "enemies of the state." Some were merely recruits who were forced to fight for the Fatherland, having been brainwashed by the vision of glory espoused by the controlling powers. Others delighted in the horrible torture and murder of Allied and Underground prisoners, never regretting their heinous crimes! According to my insight, intuition, and their answers to many questions, I had to label them as A, B, or C. If categorized as A or B they were allowed to be returned to Germany eventually without further investigation. If labelled C they were to be held longer and more research would be done by the British intelligence service into their past activities. Because of this important position I held, I was promoted to the level of captain.

According to the Geneva Convention, it was acceptable that these prisoners, who were well-fed, clothed, and given medical treatment if necessary, also were expected to participate in keeping their barracks and the grounds clean. Some were dispatched to work with nearby farmers in their fields growing and tending crops, tilling the soil, and harvesting food, as well as managing farm animals. I was also a go-between for these prisoners who often complained that they were not being fairly treated. I had to investigate any charges and come to a determination that I felt was accurate. For this reason, these prisoners considered me to be a fair arbitrator and they trusted me.

One horrifying moment for me occurred when I had to be witness to an autopsy which involved the sudden death of one of the prisoners. In the morning he was discovered dead in his bed, and malevolent designs on him had to be ruled out. It was determined that he died of a stroke but this "viewing" had a terrible effect on me, and I knew then that I could never become a doctor!

Another situation involved a handsome young prisoner who was accused of groping and sexually assaulting a girl on one of the farms. He vehemently denied the accusation but it was his word against hers. He admitted to being at that farm where he was assigned to work, and she asked him several times to assist her inside her house but he explained that he was not allowed to do that. It seemed she was vindictive about his refusal and made the accusation.

I investigated his work schedule and showed a military judge in court that on the date of the purported assault he was at a different location, and therefore he was declared not guilty. He profusely thanked me, and I became popular as a fair-minded defender.

Along with my deductive reasoning skills, I also developed a lifelong interest in cards. In England the Webbers had taught me to play whist, which has some similarities to bridge. I was looking forward to a weekend off camp but the lack of a fourth in bridge fell on me! Colonel Black deferred my leave, and when I explained that I didn't know how to play bridge he turned to Lieutenant Petrofsky, a Polish officer, and ordered him on Monday to teach me to play bridge by Friday! I fumbled through, and found a new recreation.

Immediately after the attack on Pearl Harbor, December 7, 1941, my brother Leo, dedicated to doing his part in destroying Nazism, joined the U.S. Army Air Force and he became a bombardier. His plane was one of several to bomb enemy airfields in Romania. As I noted earlier, his plane was hit, but Leo miraculously managed to parachute out along with two other Irish-American flyers. The Germans captured them, but a raid by Romanian partisans on their camp managed to get them safely out and they eventually returned to the U.S. in good shape.

The skills Leo learned in the air force and his determination to help establish the State of Israel resulted in his becoming one of the first officers in the Israeli Air Force in 1948. His lifelong friendship with his Irish-American U.S. Army Air Force pals made them willing to join with Leo in his cause. Leo eventually settled down and later married a lovely lady, Luba Bronstein from Winnipeg, who came often to Toronto to visit her relatives. He was able to get information from the Red Cross regarding our three little sisters, Erna, Josephine and Berta, and passed the news on to me, and eventually I was able to act on it.

In 1942, when the French decided they no longer wanted the Jews in Paris, most of the men had been taken away but about 12,000 women and children remained. There was a movie called *The Round-up* that describes what happened. They were kept in a crowded coliseum, in August, with no food or water. The fire brigade wanted to give them water, but the French and Germans wouldn't let them. At the orphanage, they first took away Josephine and the next week they took Erna. Berta ran after them, crying, "Please take me too! I want to go with my sisters!" but it wasn't her turn yet. She sat in the street and sobbed, but eventually returned to the orphanage. Josephine and Erna were sent by train to the Polish border and finally to Auschwitz, where they surely met an awful fate.

A defiant and fearless couple, Monsieur and Madame Strobel, were concerned about what was going on. So they went to the orphanage and took Berta home. They kept her safe during the war, claiming she was their niece from Brittany who had come to help look after their two young children, Francoise and Gerard. She attended church with them and she wore a cross, but they told her that she was really Jewish and to be silent about her true background until the war was over. These truly were the Righteous Gentiles who so honorably deserve our praise and gratitude for putting themselves in terrible danger. When I finally reunited with Berta in the recently liberated city of Paris, the Strobels told me, "We knew we could not save them all, but we felt it was our duty to try to save at least one."

Mr. Strobel was an auto mechanic, forced to repair the Nazis' vehicles. One day a high-ranking officer whose car he worked on said to him, "I understand that you have somebody looking after your children. If you ever have any problems you can call me." So even amongst the very worst people, there were some who weren't totally bad.

Also in 1942, in August, there was a train sent from Paris to Lyon with about one thousand Jewish women and children. The men in their families had previously been taken away, leaving their families vulnerable and alone. There was trouble on the tracks, so they stopped about 10 miles outside of the city. There was a church not far away, and people who saw the stopped train went to the church and told the priest that the people on the train were suffering. The priest called the Bishop of Lyon to ask what should be done. The bishop said to give them every help possible, but warned him to make sure not to end up on the train himself. One of the nuns noticed that on top of the iron bars on the rail car, there was a small space. The nun pleaded with a woman on the train, "We can't help you but if you try to push some of the babies through the gap, we promise to look after them."

The train eventually arrived in Lyon with 50 babies missing. When the French and Germans noticed, they tried to force the bishop to order the babies returned. The bishop refused, and they tried to starve him out. Eventually they took him to the Gestapo headquarters and beat him to death. There's a statue of the bishop in Lyon, memorializing him for what he did. Seventy years later, I was speaking at the Bishop Strachan School in Toronto and repeated this story. A young girl, maybe 14 years old, came to me crying and thanked me for telling the story. She said out of the 50 babies, 48 of them survived. How did she know? She was a great-niece of one of the surviving babies. She told me that many of them settled in Israel and Canada after the war.

Unfortunately, in spite of their brave actions, Berta's protectors did not fare well in France after the war. As I mentioned before, Mr. Strobel had a small auto repair shop, and during the occupation of France he was forced to work on the cars belonging to German officers. He obediently followed their orders, knowing that any objection on his part might put him, his family, and Berta in harm's way. Several years after the end of the war, a competing mechanic charged him with being a collaborator with the Germans. A case against him was brought to trial, and it made all the headlines. By that time, Berta had left the Strobels because they were planning to go to Morocco, and she (through Leo's visits to Toronto) had learned that we had a well-known philanthropist uncle, Louis Mayzel, whose family wanted to welcome and care for her in Canada.

Mr. Strobel called Berta in Toronto. At the age of 18, Berta had met and married her beloved Joseph Lunenfeld and made a life in Canada, but never forgot the wonderful adoptive family in France that helped her to survive. Berta and Joseph immediately flew to France in order to give evidence at Mr. Strobel's trial. They truthfully swore that the family protected her, risking their own lives, and any repairs on the cars owned by the Nazis had been forced on him. Ultimately, the judge condemned the accuser, and apologized to Mr. Strobel. However, the bad publicity put a stain on the Strobels and his business could not survive. Financially they were wiped out but Berta and Joe insisted on helping them get through it. Eventually they left Paris to make a new life in Morocco.

I was still living in England, interviewing German prisoners, when I reconnected with Leo and he updated me regarding our sisters. I arranged for a special leave so I could reconnect with Berta in Paris.

I had learned that the best way to be financially "flush" was to bring as many cigarettes as possible with me. I legally carried two cartons, and at the airport upon arrival, many people gave me very substantial prices for whatever I had brought!

I was overjoyed to finally be reunited with Berta. My desperate baby sister had been safely kept and had now turned into a most beautiful, happy, and well-bred young woman! I spent every minute with her and the Strobels, even being their guest for several nights. Berta was eager to spend a day alone with me, and she suggested we visit her favourite local restaurant. She ordered from the menu as she had mastered the French language in a most alluring way and ordered her favourite dish. The waiter presented me with the bill, and I asked her to check it. She was astounded to notice that the total was more than three times the usual amount! She objected about this price to the waiter who said, "What do you care? These officers have lots of money, so let them pay!" When she explained that I was her brother, the waiter retaliated with "That's what they all say!" Immediately, the owner came over, dismissed the waiter and apologized profusely to us, telling us the meal was on the house.

Paris was so exciting for me during those few good days! The Strobels took us to a famous nightclub, Le Bal Tabarin. Noted for its gaudy interior, exuberant music and especially a famous chorus line of scantily-clad mademoiselles who entertained on stage in exotic costumes, the Tabarin became the symbol of Parisian revival and victory over Nazi Germany. And how the French were delighted to celebrate! This famous club became the pivotal focus of avant-garde artists in Paris—the Futurist movement—especially Severini. Although I had become accustomed to celebratory toasts, my system could not absorb such quantities of French champagne and other delights. Consequently, just as a resounding "Here come the girls" rang out, I quickly succumbed and missed the highlight of the evening!

During these few days in Paris with my long-lost sister, we were often overwhelmed with the darkest moods as we thought about what had happened to Josephine and Erna. Berta told me how they had been taken from the orphanage, and she wept uncontrollably when she described to me how they were certainly killed along with hundreds of innocent French Jewish men, women, and children. This news had been delivered to Leo by the Red Cross, but it wasn't until years later (the fall of 2016), when I was invited through Veterans Canada to come to Prince Edward Island as a guest speaker to address schoolchildren, military nurses, cadets, and church-goers in that province, that I gained more insight into their terrible fate.

The wonderful Veterans representative in Prince Edward Island, Orlanda Drebit, had made a special trip to visit Auschwitz and her own experience of that visit was poignant and revealing. The emotions she experienced caused her to break down in tears and despair whenever her mind returned to those images. There she met an elderly Jewish lady who told her, "I was lucky that day because I was ordered to go to the kitchen and peel potatoes." Orlanda hesitatingly described to me and to others that, according to this survivor, in Auschwitz the children were awakened one morning to a blaring voice over the loudspeaker accompanied by triumphant marching music. They were told to go line up outside the barracks, and to take any toys they still had along with them. They were excited to learn they would be having showers to keep clean! "Children, take your places outside the shower room, undress, and fold your clothes at your place with any toys on top so you may recognize them when you come out." Of course, these innocents never returned.

When Orlanda described to me the horrors of their hell, we both broke down and cried because I knew finally what my dear little sisters had to go through, after all the starvation and hardship they had already endured in Vienna. My final speech in P.E.I. was at the local church, and the most beautiful hymns and Second World War songs were sung by their famous travelling choir. At the conclusion, instead of having Orlanda make her expression of thanks to me, I requested that she retell this heartbreaking story to the congregation. Her exact words follow:

"Today I glimpsed into the abyss of madness, which was Hitler's regime. That humans are capable of smiling and laughing, as they led rabbis, priests, women, children and men to their death, is beyond comprehension. That the most educated nation in Europe could commit such horrors is beyond belief! May the incalculable suffering of those who perished in these death camps, cry out to be forever preserved and may God have mercy on their souls."

When she concluded, the entire audience stood in silence, heads bowed. As they filed out of the church, each took my hand and blessed us. One father said his young daughter wanted to ask me a question. "Of course," I responded.

"How old were your two little sisters when they died in the concentration camp?" As I looked at this little girl, I answered, "Ten and twelve years old." She gasped and clung to her father's arm, exclaiming, "I am twelve years old, will the bad people come and get me?"

My immediate response was to soothe her fears, explaining, "No, my dear one; you are protected by your family and the brave soldiers keeping guard over all of us to ensure that this never happens again. We promote love and tolerance for all good people and trust that our government and leaders will keep us safe." She hugged me. "Those brave men and women fought and died so we, the future generations, could enjoy our freedom!"

When we left P.E.I., we thanked our hosts Ann and Dwayne MacEwen and also the gracious hotel staff who cared for us so well.

Returning to England in 1946, my duties at the prison camp were about to be concluded after almost one full year. Destiny again intervened, and I took on a new challenge. I was invited to join a team of lawyers and several interpreters of different languages—German, Russian, Polish, etc.—to go to Washington, D.C., to study thousands of documents relating to General von Rundstedt, Overcommander of the Western front, pertaining to his Commando Order which stated the following:

"If you capture Allied soldiers who are wearing the Red Berets of the Airborne Division, or the Green Berets of the Commando Division, do not take them prisoner, but shoot them immediately."

The hope was that we would uncover documents to provide the proof necessary to try him in court for war crimes.

Our journey to North America was on the prestigious British ship the *Queen Mary*; it had been converted from a passenger ship to a troop ship for war purposes. As officers, we still travelled two to a cabin, but were given many advantages in service and food. Evenings were filled with entertainment and musical presentations, many from amateur performers. However, some very special notables were sailing with us—in particular, Ella Fitzgerald (who volunteered to sing) and the British film director Alfred Hitchcock on his way to Hollywood.

We finally arrived in New York, and were transported by train to Washington where we were met by a dozen attractive young female representatives and taken to our hotel. We were extremely popular, as there was an obviously dire shortage of men, and people seemed to be in a particularly celebratory mood. As this was August 1946, not many places were air-conditioned, but those that were advertised the fact most blatantly. The Pentagon, where we were working, was delightfully cool, as was our hotel, but the heat and humidity outdoors was extremely uncomfortable.

I had an American corporal assigned to me. He was to bring me any documents written in German that were relevant to the case against von Rundstedt. It was my job to carefully review these papers, mark and translate their contents, and hand them over to my assistant to be typed up and then verified once more by me.

Incidentally this U.S. corporal was paid more than twice as much as I was as a British captain. My salary was augmented by the government by $10 a day for food allowance and necessities. We frequented various restaurants, but our favourite was the Italian one offering a 99-cent special of spaghetti and meatballs, plus 25 cents for a tip.

Each day we worked diligently until we amassed a mountain of evidence against the corrupt general. Many of these discoveries were extremely upsetting to us, as they revealed unheard-of cruelties and hardship. In particular, one of the Russian interpreters came upon a document referencing his own small town where the Germans killed everyone, including his own immediate and extended family members.

Another one of the interpreters had his own special story. As a German-born Jew in the British army, he looked the part of a true Christian German, tall with blonde hair and blue eyes. He was given the documents and passport of a particular German officer whom he resembled and who was killed in the Russian campaign. Arrangements were made for him to connect with two German anti-Nazi engineers to eventually locate and interrupt a heavy-water installation outside Berlin. They successfully blew up this essential scientific laboratory, thus delaying the manufacturing of the atomic bomb by Germany. He eventually escaped to Switzerland where the border guards arrested him, but he was rescued by British officials who paid a substantial amount in gold to get him back.

After two years of work, and more than sufficient evidence for a trial against the German General von Rundstedt for his war crimes, the pronouncement that we would not be able to proceed against him brought us great frustration and disappointment. Because of the Berlin Blockade by Russia, food and supplies could only reach its population by plane (via parachute). Both America and Britain were convinced that they needed the Germans to fight "Russian control," so it was announced that General von Rundstedt, at the age of 65, was too old and too sick to be tried.

We, the victors, with all the evidence of his crimes, had to drop the case. All the time, energy, and evidence needed to bring von Rundstedt to justice was cast away. We were inconsolable with this decision but had to accept it. He was let go, a free man to live in peace, never having to pay for his horrible crimes!

While living in Washington I was working diligently, patiently and thoroughly going over details of crimes that took place during World War II. My life was not all "donkey work" or intelligence investigations, though. Many "liberated" and brilliant, attractive young women were eager to meet young Allied officers, and my friends and I never lacked for female company. But I hesitated to make any formal commitment with anyone due to my uncertain future, and memories of family hardship in my past.

A particular event hardened my outlook and gave me the impetus to tell my personal story to promote tolerance and understanding for others. Two State Department lawyers with whom I was friendly and I decided we needed a well-deserved rest on an upcoming weekend. We had heard about a nearby resort and hotel in Virginia Beach that was recommended, and I booked three rooms under my name, Captain Martin Maxwell. When we arrived at the hotel, all eager to relax and enjoy the vacation, I signed in and so did my other two companions.

There seemed to be some problem with their accommodations; when the hotel desk manager explained that they had only one room under Maxwell, I presented my confirmation slip showing reservations for three rooms. She surreptitiously tried to explain that "we don't rent rooms to those kinds…" My friends Abe Goldberg and Sam Stein glared angrily, and we immediately left the hotel. It wasn't until we reached the end of the path to the road on our way out that we noticed the sign indicating "no Jews or dogs allowed here." This event happened after the war's ending, and the horrific discovery of the concentration camps.

My memoirs would not be complete if I omitted a most precious moment of my time in Washington. This was my "accidental" but contrived meeting with Harry S. Truman, the Democrat who was re-elected president in 1948 after succeeding Franklin D. Roosevelt upon the latter's death in 1945.

Along with a group of supporters for Truman, wanting to show approval of him and hoping to catch a glimpse of this great man, I waited at a specific location on the street in Washington. We all knew that his routine took him this way for his daily walk from Blair House. As he approached me, his two Secret Service officers prevented me from using my camera. However, as I was in uniform, Truman stepped forward and asked me directly, "What are you doing in Washington?" When I explained, he continued with more inquiries, asking my name and about my service during the war. He then shook my hand and thanked me for my service, and allowed me to take his picture.

Ten days later I received an invitation to attend his inauguration parade, and I sat approximately ten feet away from him. Shortly after, our mission was ended, and I was returned to England without accomplishing what I came to America to do. At this point in my life, I made a decision to resign from the Army, and to return to civilian life to live with the Webbers.

CHAPTER SIX

Return to Civilian Life

My relief about my miraculous survival during the war and my confidence in being given important decision-making positions were tempered by the social environment in England. The war had almost depleted Britain's finances, and the adjustment to a new set of norms was a challenge for every Briton. Women had gained independence and were now ready to take on jobs that previously had been held only by men. Social class still played a strong role in determining one's "place" in society, but servitude and obedience among the lower levels of society began to erode as women and men became more educated and skilled in specialized careers. During my absence from England, the voice of Winston Churchill (the driving force for victory during the war) was muted as the Labour Party led by Clement Attlee gained power. England was certainly changing!

Mr. Webber, skilled in furniture repair and in polishing the finished product, was given additional work for a recognized and large company called Freeland. His son Laurie was assisting him in this, as was I, but we both sought more sophisticated full-time employment. An ad from Marks and Spencer caught my eye, as they were looking for a junior salesperson whom they were willing to train. I was interviewed by a well-dressed and solicitous young man about my own age. He asked me several questions regarding politics, my job in the Army, and my general ability to learn several aspects of selling and dealing with the public. At the conclusion, he explained his decision to turn me down. It was because I did not have a university degree! I explained that my last six years were spent in the Army, and then I pointedly asked him, "Why weren't you in the Army?" But I received no reply.

This did not deter me in my search for a job, but many years later when Marks and Spencer was considering opening stores in Canada, I met one of their top executives. At this point I was a successful business owner. I retold the anecdote of my job interview and he said, "Too bad he didn't hire you." Jokingly he added, "You may have been president of the company by now!"

I continued in my search for an interesting and challenging job, but my main objective was to earn a salary to provide for myself and also to help support the Webbers. They needed a small cutting machine for their furniture business, but they never put any pressure on me to help out. Consequently, I applied to be a waiter in the only kosher restaurant in Manchester, owned by two rabbis. At that time there were 60,000 Jews in Manchester, many in the textile business and in prominent careers. They were mostly very Orthodox and this was really the sole restaurant where they could get a kosher meal "out." Lunchtime started at 11:30 a.m. and ran till 2 p.m., but by 11 a.m. crowds were lined up outside. At the counters and tables, patrons waited behind customers already eating, to ensure their place next as soon as the first individual finished his meal. The most popular dish was fish and chips. One day at lunchtime, as a customer was about to delve into his preferred meal, he was suddenly called away. "Dr. Katz, please come to the pharmacy immediately!" came over the loudspeaker. As soon as the gentleman got up, the waiting customer behind him sat down and finished the meal for him! Dr. Katz had to patiently wait for his order to be prepared and served again.

Life at the restaurant was chaotic, but I enjoyed meeting the families who frequented it and as a result became more involved in the

Jewish social life of the city. Due to my hard work and diligence, this menial job was rewarding as most people gave me excellent tips. However, each waiter had to hand over 15 percent of his tips to the head waiter, who unfortunately frittered it away gambling.

I learned other lessons. The restaurant hired a wonderful pastry maker. But not all of his desserts reached the customers. He often prepared delicious delicacies, and instead of serving them in the restaurant, placed them outside the back door near the garbage disposal where his friend picked them up "gratis" to be served and charged in his catering business. In spite of this, the restaurant was very successful and the two rabbis made substantial profits.

In appreciation, the rabbis provided me with excellent letters of reference, which I added to other letters I had received from dignitaries in the army. I was constantly in touch with my brother Leo, and he advised me that my sister Berta was now in Canada and would be getting married soon. This spurred me on to make a difficult decision. As much as I loved my adoptive Webber family, I felt the need to join my sister in Toronto and to be close to my brother in the U.S. border city of Detroit. As I investigated the means to go to North America, there was only one date open to me. I had to decide quickly or this singular opportunity would be gone.

June weddings were planned for both Laurie, my adoptive brother, and for my sister Berta. Fate made it impossible to attend either one! I would have to leave too early to stay for Laurie and his fiancé Frieda Isaacson's wedding, but I would arrive too late for Berta's. The *Queen Mary* was no longer a troop ship but a renovated passenger ship—accommodations were fair, but the food was excellent.

I arrived in Canada first at the port of entry in Halifax, then travelled by train to Toronto. A great celebration followed my arrival there. Greeted by Berta and her new husband, Joseph Lunenfeld, the family we had never known consisted of two Mayzel (Maisel) brothers, Louis and Moishe, their wives and children, and a host of cousins. This welcoming group of relatives gave me a warm-hearted greeting, somehow easing the pain of the loss of my very dear immediate family.

Berta had been living with Louis and Simcha Mayzel until she married Joe in the newly-built Beth Sholom synagogue on Eglinton Avenue. Joe's family mostly lived in Brantford, Ontario, and they were so delighted with his choice of a bride. Berta and Joe invited me to stay with them until I could get established and she soon happily announced that she was about to be a mother. We resided in a tiny two-bedroom apartment near the top of Yonge Street at what was then the city limit. At this point, the Yonge streetcar would turn around and proceed back southbound to downtown Toronto.

The voyage across the Atlantic and my other expenses depleted my resources. I was determined to find any temporary job to get me through the first few weeks in Canada. I searched the want ads section of the newspaper, along with another ex-serviceman I met on the ship. Since I firmly believe that any job is a beginning and better than no job, I resorted to washing cars at a location on Spadina Avenue. This barely got me through to my next placement. Workers were required for a seed company—Biggs' Seeds. My friend was even more desperate than I was. Pre-war, he had been a farmer, so this ad appealed to him. He called me from Union Station, telling me he was broke, and he asked me if he could borrow some money to tide him over. I willingly lent him what I could for some food and we were both optimistic about the new job possibility.

Arriving at the Biggs' location, the foreman explained that he needed large bags of seeds carried to a watering truck. Instructed to turn our backs to him, he flung two large, heavy bags onto our backs. It didn't take more than two seconds and four steps for both of us to fall down. My friend weighed only 118 lbs. and I weighed even less. The foreman said, "Sorry boys, this job is not for you" and he sympathetically handed each of us a quarter to subsidize our trip back on the streetcar.

Scouring the ads again, I noticed that a possible job for my friend and his girlfriend (whom he later married) was miraculously in sight—"Cheese-maker and housekeeper wanted" at a nearby farm. As he had experience in this area, he immediately contacted the dairy farmer. The farmer forwarded him the money needed to travel to the farm, and my heart was lightened by this good luck. This chance placement encouraged me to keep looking for myself.

The employment agency informed me of a job at Lever Brothers on Eastern Avenue. It was not a challenging position but I was glad to take it. Another young man and I were asked to paint the walls and ceiling of a large warehouse in the heat of summer with no air conditioning. We worked diligently in 100 degree Fahrenheit heat in our underwear. They informed us that several other applicants had given up, so they admired our persistence. Next, they offered me the menial job of dropping a dishcloth into an open box of "Rinso" soap powder on the assembly line. This job was boring, but it paid!

Elated about my first big paycheck of about $200, I boarded the Yonge streetcar, ready to repay my sister for her faith in me!

Now the worst thing happened. As I neared my stop, I noticed my pay envelope was missing! How despondent I was at this loss, but my continued optimism of some goodness in people came to the fore when that evening an elderly gentleman, reading the name and address on the envelope, came to our door and was happy to return it to me. I offered him a small reward but he refused, saying, "This belongs to you. Maybe one day you will have the chance to help someone in need, so promise me you will do so!"

Several weeks later, a notice appeared on the Lever Brothers billboard advertising an opening for two salesmen in another department. "If interested, please arrange an appointment where you will be introduced to the management and a test will be given to you." I was immediately excited about this possibility and I came back on Saturday morning to be interviewed, along with hundreds of others.

The written test took two hours, and the interview was short but encouraging. The following Sunday I was called and told that I came in second place! Not bad for a recent immigrant whose first language was German. The next day, after congratulating me, Mr. Smithers (an executive) asked me to fill in some family background. This included family names of my relatives. Truth began to emerge about the necessity of this questionnaire as questions regarding religion on an employment form were not allowed. Smithers quickly glanced at the responses and standing up announced, "Thank you, we'll be in touch."

On the following Wednesday at a board meeting, Mr. McLaughlin asked why only one winning participant attended. Smithers responded, "I didn't hire the other one because he's Jewish." It appeared that with over 200 applicants, not one was Jewish aside from me. A World War II veteran at the table, Major Collins, read my resume and said, "If you do not hire Mr. Maxwell, I will resign and personally go to every newspaper in Canada to expose your bigotry. As you know, we have many Jewish pharmacists across the country and you can bet what their response will be when they learn about this unacceptable practice!"

The committee quickly decided to do the right thing and they hired me. I'm certain they never regretted the decision, as I became a top salesman, selling to Towers Department Store, Woolworths, Kresge, and many other chains.

CHAPTER SEVEN

Sharing My Experiences

Now that I felt more secure in Canada with my well-paying job, I was able to move into my own quarters—a basement apartment in a family home. The widowed mother of three teenagers was happy to have the additional income and a refined Jewish gentleman living downstairs. Lever Brothers gave me a car and expense money, and I now had time to participate in community events and get to know more of the family. After what I had been through, I wanted to help others in need as I had been so gratefully assisted.

I heard about the organization B'nai Brith, to which my cousin Leonard Mayzel belonged. These young men were dedicated to maintaining a strong social connection with members, who were happy to assist in areas in the Toronto community that could benefit. This group was called Ontario Lodge. We ran and organized a weekly bingo game with all money raised going to local charities. Leonard, a recent pharmacy graduate, and another friend from the Lodge, Al Feingold, an optometry graduate, planned a driving trip to Western Canada. They invited me to join them. Lever Brothers granted me 10 days of holiday and our plans were made. When I became ill with a raging fever, my plans to join them were cancelled. However, they could not postpone their outbound trip, so the two of them went together.

As fate would have it, along the way the car hit a slippery patch and went out of control, rolling down a ravine, resulting in the instant death of Leonard. This tragedy struck us all. Al was injured, and recovered slowly. The Lodge changed its name to honour one of the founders, becoming the Leonard Mayzel Ontario Lodge, and continued to do good in the community. This Lodge provided a yearly event for the disabled children in the Bloorview Home; they distributed Christmas and Hanukkah baskets to needy families and sponsored a desperate cerebral palsy victim, Charles. They made sure he was taken in his wheelchair to all our meetings and social events. In later years, we also sent greetings and gift baskets to our Canadian troops in Afghanistan.

With the popularity of the Lodge, its numbers swelled to over 300. Eventually, in 1966, I became president of the Leonard Mayzel Lodge. The monthly Lodge bulletin soon was headed, "The President Takes a Wife," for I gladly put down roots in Toronto and married the love of my life, Eleanor, whom I had met at a dance my first year in the Lodge.

It is an ideal situation in life when an employee enjoys the job, and I certainly did! The social connections in the pharmacy business and the satisfaction of being one of Lever Brothers' top salesmen made me very happy. I was an accepted member of society, with close ties to my family here, and I developed many lifelong friendships. One of my favourite customers was the affable and entrepreneurial Ed Mirvish, owner of Honest Ed's. Before I contacted him, he had never before carried products from Lever Brothers. Ed's friendly and likable buyer, John Soltisek, always greeted me with a hearty handshake and a big smile as we enjoyed our monthly lunch in a nearby restaurant on Bloor Street.

As my reputation grew, many of the drug store owners urged me to try starting a new business of my own. They recognized my potential and trustworthiness, but at that time I lacked the capital for such a venture.

One particular incident in my sales career comes to mind. One cold November morning I had just entered a drug store on St. Clair Avenue near Bathurst Street. The owner, all on his own, was unable to leave the store and asked me if I would get him a cup of coffee. As I walked back into the blistering wind, I noticed a man huddled against the wall; he was wearing only a thin coat and looked very pale. He asked me if I could give him some change for a hot coffee. I quickly surmised he was quite desperate and I yelled, "Follow me!"

In the restaurant I saw the daily special—orange juice, toast, bacon, eggs and coffee for 79 cents (this was reasonable, even in 1956!). I left enough extra for a small tip and then took the pharmacist's coffee back to him. Four weeks later when I returned to the pharmacy, I entered the diner and asked the waitress if they ever saw that poor man again. Yes, she stated. As he had thankfully finished his breakfast, the chef came out and yelled in frustration, "Our dishwasher called, he's unable to come in today." He turned to our customer and asked for his assistance, offering him as well a place to stay on a cot upstairs in the hall if he needed it.

I asked if he was still around. Surprisingly, a young man came out, explaining he recently came here from Newfoundland, had become ill and spent many months in the hospital. His belongings at the boarding house were disposed of and he had spent the night before I met him sleeping in an open van parked nearby.

The chef took a liking to him and later helped him go to cooking school. Sixteen years had elapsed when I received a letter from this "bum." He wrote that he wanted to thank me but was unable to find me prior to then. The pharmacy had closed and the restaurant changed hands but he was finally able to contact someone who knew me. He continued, telling me of his good fortune. "I met a wonderful woman. We now have two children, a home, a car, and I have a good job as a chef in a fine restaurant. Thanks to you for being so concerned, and buying me a breakfast."

I remembered the hard-working baker in Vienna who treated me with respect and was concerned when I was hungry, and his telling me to have compassion and help others whenever I could. I often retell this story to students, so they begin to understand how each small deed may be of great importance.

As I became more knowledgeable in the sales of pharmaceutical products, and more secure in my ability to sell and distribute many items, I began to think about self-employment. At the urging of many friends in the business and after learning of many success stories, I decided to take a chance and go into business on my own. I gave my notice to Lever Brothers, asking how much time they needed me to stay on in order to train a new recruit. They were sorry to have me leave, but I did go on the best of terms, remaining friendly with them for many years. My pension money was withdrawn as I needed it for weekly expenses.

My head was full of ideas, but my first priority was for a bank loan in order to purchase saleable items. The bank manager interviewed me, and agreed with a handshake to lend me $3,000. With no collateral on my side, he stated that he had read about my service in the British Army in my resume and was impressed sufficiently to show his confidence in me. "I lend money to people, not to companies, and I know you will be successful," he said. My landlady at home allowed me to store several items in her garage, and this was a beginning. Next, I required warehouse space to hold more items, and found a valuable friend in Mr. Phil White, who offered me empty space in the basement of his pharmacy at no charge. Mr. White later became the Reeve of York Township and was highly respected for his contributions to the area.

Along with my young nephew, Allan Lunenfeld, and his sister Suzy, we cleaned Mr. White's basement and put up shelving. The payoff for their labour was a big hamburger and drink each from the newly opened Harvey's Hamburgers on Dufferin Street. My first sale was two dozen pairs of sunglasses, which I sold for $16. I still have the receipt, framed.

A new product, Penaten baby cream from Germany, had made its debut at Hilary's Drug Store on Dundas at Bathurst. This remarkable product cured baby diaper rash. When my sister Berta gave birth to Ruthy, the doctor had recommended Penaten and it was effective. Mr. Hilary was the sole importer of this wonder drug, and I sold it into Lever Brothers.

As my business grew, the space in the basement became too small. I searched for more room to hold the growing number of items— shampoos, mouthwash, sunglasses, toothbrushes, etc. I thanked Mr. White and then rented part of a warehouse space on Bentworth Avenue. When the original owners decided to move further north, these Italian-Canadian landlords and businessmen offered me part of the space at the amazing price of one dollar per square foot, for 5,000 square feet. What a bargain!

After attending a trade show in Montreal, I became interested in the importing and production of packaged cotton balls, and eventually purchased sufficient raw material for the owners to send me the raw cotton balls and the machines, as they wanted to be partners in the venture I would run. I agreed. Eventually this became a very successful business, requiring two secretaries, a bookkeeper, a warehouse manager, and up to 23 factory workers. My contacts with Honest Ed's, Loblaws, and Towers Stores were firm and continued with great success.

My marriage, late in my life at age 42, was very satisfying. My devoted wife Eleanor found her work as a teacher challenging and intellectually stimulating. Both incomes combined to help us buy a home. Later, our two teenage sons, Brian and Randy, were developing into responsible adults, and we began to be able to afford travel and trips to Florida for short periods of time. My mother-in-law, Florence Ross, was especially grateful for her "favourite son-in-law" and she lived with us for many years. Although we continued our membership at the Beth Sholom synagogue on Eglinton Avenue, we were not ardent devotees who attended every Sabbath; however, our ties to the faith remained firm. With success in business and reliable, devoted staff at work, I was able to take several trips and cruises. Early in 1966 I had travelled to Israel, and was able to return multiple times to witness the miracle G–d had promised us.

One trip was a visit to Vienna. This was sponsored by a Jewish organization led by an amazing gentleman, himself a survivor of seven concentration camps! Our hosts welcomed back any children, now adults, who were able to leave on the Kindertransport from Austria. We stayed at a fine hotel in Vienna and met many dignitaries at the Rathskeller, and executives in old, established insurance and banking corporations. The hostess for this return visit was Mrs. Mariott, who also introduced us to the thriving Orthodox Jewish Community and took us to a particular school which accepted only children with special academic status. It was explained to us that many of those gifted children and teachers were forced to leave the school, as they were Jewish. Subsequently, a special stone with the names of these students and teachers was inscribed, and placed in a prominent location on the grounds in deference to their memories and their contributions. A memorial statement was made when the current principal introduced himself before I was about to speak. It was relevant to me that in his apology he admitted: "We, the Austrians, must realize and accept our communal guilt in the tragedy. We must no longer 'sweep under the rug' the fact that Austria welcomed Hitler." This admission was a first step to try to reach some form of reconciliation. Mrs. Mariott also arranged for us to visit the Jewish cemetery where we were able to locate my parents' graves, neglected and overgrown with weeds although my brother Leo had sent monthly payments for their upkeep from Detroit. On my return to Canada, I arranged the repair of their markers and insisted that photographs be taken to prove their upkeep. I often wonder if the tragedy of their early deaths and the dispersal of our small family perhaps saved them from the horrible inevitability of the death camps.

Somehow, even with our charitable activities in the community, I felt something was missing but I was reluctant to return to images of my unhappy childhood and the horrible events I witnessed during the war. However, a particular incident spurred me on to take part in bringing the "Jewish condition" in our society into focus for better understanding and tolerance. At that time, my very proficient and professional secretary Flora announced that she was about to get married to a fine young British-Canadian businessman. Flora was Chinese-Canadian, and both families were happy about the forthcoming union.

The wedding was a big event, with a sumptuous meal, music, and dancing at a large venue. Seated at our table were several couples whom I had not met before. A burly chap, a friend of the groom, began a conversation with me and, noticing my accent, asked me where I came from and about my participation during the war. He blurted out, "I suppose you were shielded in England, and were safely provided for by doing some office work or another easy job to avoid meaningful participation during the war years, like most Jews." Before I had an opportunity to respond, another guest at our table immediately jumped up and grabbed him with two hands around his collar. He said firmly, "You must apologize to Mr. Maxwell! Not only did he sign up early before he was even allowed, but he participated in two major campaigns of the war, D-Day and Arnhem, and made a great contribution, but was injured severely and placed in a prisoner-of-war camp! You owe a great deal to men like him, and you must never presume that a newcomer to England, one of the Jewish faith, was shirking his duty!" The denouncer then took his seat, apologized to me and left early, embarrassed.

My opportunity to make some positive contribution came when

I met Reverend Nelson, pastor of the "Christian-Jewish Dialogue." This wonderful organization brings together people of different faiths and through meetings and talks, promotes better understanding while focusing on eliminating detrimental stereotypes and imagery such as those promoted by the Nazis. Several weeks after I joined, Reverend Nelson called me in desperation. "Please do me a big favour." There was a terrible storm across the city, and it was very dark outside. "We are at a church on the Kingsway and I have a full audience waiting to hear from a Holocaust survivor who became ill and cannot attend. Will you please come right away and speak?" I called on a friend, Bernie Burstyn, an educated and ordained Rabbi who was not employed with any particular synagogue at that time. Bernie came to the rescue and we found our way to the waiting audience.

I had not prepared a speech, but spoke from the heart. When I finished my story, I received an unbelievable standing ovation. The Reverend told me, "You must not waste this opportunity and your ability to deliver this message. You should take every speaking opportunity you can get ... schools, churches, synagogues, club meetings and to veterans!" I reached out to the youth at many prestigious schools—Upper Canada College, Branksome Hall, Centennial College, St. Andrew's, Bishop Strachan, and the Crestwood School, whose history teacher, Scott Masters, promotes and lives the life of an ardent historian and supporter of Holocaust education in order to prevent any other such disasters. At the York School, I was overwhelmed when the principal called to tell me that since I was prevented from receiving my high school diploma in 1938 when Jewish students were forced to leave Austria, they wanted to grant me an honorary diploma from their school. At the age of 80, I could finally say that I had my diploma, and the students, teachers and my family all attended the ceremony.

Over the years I continued with all the strength I had, to speak in Britain while on a visit to the grandchildren of the Webbers, in the U.S. when I visited during the winter months, in Vienna with a group who were on the Kindertransport, and especially in Holland where I was honoured at a sporting venue by a huge congregation that included the Dutch Royal Family. I have been welcomed by veteran groups in Sydney, Nova Scotia and in Prince Edward Island. Some of my greatest welcomes occurred when I addressed the United Church in Barrie, Ontario, and at Camp Borden, as well as the Ontario Provincial Police in Orillia, Ontario, where the auditorium was filled to capacity with new recruits and working police officers, with a simulcast hook-up that reached several thousand more.

My most memorable venture was the first opportunity for me and a fellow B'nai Brith member, Norman Horenfelt, to go as delegates to Israel in early 1966. We were so excited and thrilled to see the early years of this struggling state, and I marveled at the determination of Israelis who deserve great credit in clearing desert lands, bringing water to undeveloped areas, creating universities and maintaining medical research facilities. All this while fending off constant attacks from neighbouring Arab states. I remembered how my 50 groschen in Vienna, along with thousands of others, went into the little blue boxes, and the words of the baker who predicted that we would someday have a land of our own which would continually require forbearance and protection in order to survive.

Personal anecdotes which may be happenstance or purely coincidental make me a relevant observer of a special moment in time and place. Another delegate, who managed to arrive in the U.S. and had lost his entire family, decided against his doctor's advice to take a chance and visit Israel. He felt comfortable being with me and Norman (another Canadian) because he had a slight German accent. As our group entered a narrow passageway into the Knesset he seemed to recognize another elderly man on the other side of the room. Pushing us aside, he moved to the fore and said, "I must go closer; that man resembles members of my late family!" As he approached, the other gentleman looked up in complete surprise to yell, "You are my long lost brother whom I could never find and I presumed was dead!" The brother had survived the war, now lived in Brazil and had determined that he, too, would visit Israel! What are the chances that two brothers now living in different countries visited Israel and at the same moment entered the same building and as a result were able to meet their destiny and live out the rest of their lives with an amazing bond of love for each other?

My personal quest was to try and locate other members of my own family whom I had learned now lived in Israel. Telephones were scarce, but after several attempts I found someone in Haifa who knew about the Meisels family that had come to Israel from Syria. There, I connected with the family of Yossi Meisels, and from then on I began to have a close friendship with another cousin, Zvi Mazel, who now lived in Jerusalem. Zvi and his wife Michelle became prominent figures in educational and diplomatic circles. Zvi was the first Israeli ambassador to go to Egypt under Sadat's regime. His son, Shlomo, was able to celebrate his Bar Mitzvah in Cairo when Sadat agreed to re-open the synagogue there for that event. Zvi also continued his duties in Romania and in Sweden and now has retired, living in Jerusalem once again. We were fortunate to be able to visit them and the close family there, along with two of our adult grandchildren when we took a cruise in 2017 that stopped in Israel for several days.

As I became more comfortable financially in my business, I was able to depend more and more on the devoted managers of National Home Products. We had a very close family relationship, and they never let me down. My employees always stayed on for many years and I showed my appreciation for their loyalty and trustworthiness. I now had the liberty to travel more, and contemplated reaching out to different communities to tell my personal story and to help others appreciate the sacrifices that were made by so many in order for us to keep our freedom.

In England, while visiting the Webber family, I spoke to students in Leeds; in the U.S., my talks were given in schools in Florida and, in particular, at a famous golf and country club in Los Angeles for a large fundraising event. My only request was for expenses for my wife and myself. As I became more known, I was asked to speak on Cape Breton Island and, as mentioned earlier, through Veterans Affairs we met a very appreciative audience in Prince Edward Island. We remain in touch with our charming hosts, Duane and Ann MacEwen. As well, Calgary's Jewish Community gave me a hearty welcome.

In particular, my war experiences drew me to strongly consider visiting Holland. The opportunity to do so came at the sixtieth anniversary of the country's liberation. We had not been able to attend the fiftieth anniversary reunion, so we were determined to make it this time. This was the country so devastated during the war years. This was the land of Anne Frank, and where many Jewish children had been saved by brave and courageous Dutch people. This was where starving hundreds fought in the underground to keep the spirit alive. And this was the land where so many of us had been injured or killed, or managed to survive the desperate conditions in the prisoner-of-war camps.

When I excitedly applied to attend the ceremonies through Veterans Affairs, a wonderful family (the Van De Sandes, who lived in Apeldoorn) wanted in particular to host a Jewish war veteran. They were concerned about the details of our need for kosher food, or if we would be disturbed by having young children around! We met and made fast friends of this gracious couple who gave up their bedroom to us and moved onto their children's beds, with the children sleeping on bed rolls in the attic. The only daunting experience with them was the nightly climb up the narrow stairs. Els, Mrs. Van De Sande, was a medical doctor on a senior faculty nearby, and Berend was the editor of the local edition of the newspaper in Amsterdam.

As we were written about each day, we were feted by all of their neighbours and friends.

One of the great and exciting challenges made to the neighbouring streets and towns was to put up the best decorations for the Liberation Remembrances. Every house, every tree, and each window greeted us with decorations. Canadian, British and American flags were so abundant that the stores ran out! Streamers hung from each lamppost, Dutch chocolates were given freely as well as keychains with small Dutch clogs. The residents of the winning street actually placed stuffed dummies replicating British airmen, tied in place in the trees, laden with boxes of food and other provisions. We all drank special liqueurs to toast the winners—they wouldn't let us go!

On this remembrance, we solemnly visited the famous cemetery in Oosterbeek. We were greeted by the Queen Beatriz, who especially welcomed the veterans with grateful thanks. She stated, at the end of a moving ceremony: "Thank you for coming today in May to celebrate our freedom, and especially thank you for coming so many years ago to fight with us, to give us back our freedom that we almost lost."

During the sixtieth anniversary of the Liberation, our reception was unbelievable. Over 200,000 people, including roughly 10,000 children, lined the streets to greet our parade as we were comfortably seated in open Jeeps. They reached out to touch us, shaking our hands and inundating us with bouquets of flowers.

As our parade temporarily halted, I noticed a particular lovely blonde-haired girl of about twelve pushing her way forward insistently to get close to our van. She shook my hand, presented me with candy, flowers and a letter. As our procession moved slowly forward, she fell back into the crowd. Alongside us on bicycles were members of the worldwide press and television. They, of course, noticed the young girl's presentation to me, and several of them asked me to reveal the contents of the letter! I opened the envelope and read the words to us all.

"A long, long time ago you came and fought for our freedom. Many died, but thankfully you saved my Omah (grandmother) who was sick and hungry. You gave her medicine and food. More food was dropped from your planes. You saved us! That is why I am here today, to shake your hand and say 'Thank you!'"

This episode was replayed on Canadian and world television several times over the next few days.

Our final emotional event of the visit was to the Arnhem Oosterbeek War Cemetery, where we fought in September 1944. No less than 1700 of our division, the British 1st Airborne, are buried there. Crosses, Stars of David with names, and the saddest, with no religious marker, just "Here Lies a Soldier." One grave marked with a Star of David had inscribed on it, "He fought and died so his people might live."

I left some small stones on another Jewish grave because I recognized the name. On December 31 in 1938, this paratrooper as a child was with me on the Kindertransport train from Vienna to England. As I stood there, remembering him, I thanked the warm-hearted and wonderful British people of 1938–39 for welcoming 10,000 Jewish children when nobody else wanted us.

The visit in my own mind was incomplete as I searched for something special—a message from these young brave soldiers to touch us today and always. I found it in the simple phrase inscribed on a nearby headstone. "When you go home, tell them of us and say, 'For your tomorrow, we gave our today.'"

On the seventy-fifth anniversary of D-Day, June 6, 2019, I placed a wreath in the commemorative service attended by many dignitaries here in Toronto, and I remembered those precious words. I considered the world at that moment, so far in the future from the Second World War but still somewhat resembling the past: the violence and attacks on churches, synagogues, mosques and private citizens, the loss of hope, and the despair we all feel when we hear about them. If those young men could rise and see the state of our world now, they would grieve in anguish, "What the hell did you do with the tomorrows we gave you?"

A few days after the ceremony, a Member of Parliament, Mr. Brassard in Barrie, Ontario, contacted me to ask my permission to read this part of my speech from the D-Day service in Parliament. Of course, I obliged him. He read it twice and a moment of silent reverence was observed afterward.

Now to the previous final farewell at the Sport Palace in Apeldoorn in 2015. After speeches and thank you's accompanied by rousing marches and Second World War favourites played by the band, the veterans were asked to file out and follow the Princess as she was leaving with the rest of the Royal Family. To the resonant tune of Vera Lynn's famous wartime song, we joined in the singing of "We'll Meet Again." There were tears in the eyes of many of the Dutch onlookers as well as the vets, as everyone was aware this could likely be their last parade.

Due to security protocols, only the veterans were allowed into the special reception room (no wives or other family members). The Princess asked me to come over, took a photo with me, and spoke to me briefly. "I remember everything you spoke about the last time you were here, and when you handed over the Torch of Freedom from your generation to our grandchildren's generation. You said, 'There are so few of us left.'" And I say now as I said then: I am handing over the Torch of Freedom. Hold it high so everyone can see how precious freedom is. And if ever you have to fight for it, do it with all your might, because once it is lost it is almost impossible to get it back. It took us five years, and millions of injured and dead to regain it to give you, the Dutch and the world, that freedom which is so precious. G–d bless both our countries, the Netherlands and Canada, and G–d bless us all!

My closing thoughts are a mix of memories and tremendous gratitude to those who perished so that we might live. To the caregivers and providers of today—scientists, nurses, doctors, delivery people, food producers and our responsible leaders in government who bear the heavy burden of decision-making. To the struggling families in wartime Britain who sheltered me, and especially to the Webber family and, in Paris, the Strobels who concealed my sister Berta Lunenfeld. To the army, for comradeship and discipline. To my special welcome in Canada, where I was able to join my remaining family and build a new and fulfilling life—Canada, land of diversity, freedom, and opportunity for all.

Thanks, that in my lifetime I saw the birth of Israel and that I was able to visit the land of Biblical Promise. It continues to survive and give to the world medical advances and Tikkun Olam (altruism). And especially thanks for the friendships and assistance of so many, particularly my devoted employees, so that I was able to live my tomorrows today and experience regeneration in the life of newborn members of our family.

AFTERWORD

A Visit to Vienna

Martin Maxwell wrote this account of his return to Vienna around 1975.

The Cook's tour bus with 40 English-speaking tourists was travelling through the outskirts of Vienna. Long-forgotten landmarks and street names came back to my memory. As the guide extolled the beauty of Vienna and pointed out some of the beautiful buildings, it seemed impossible to me that nearly forty years had gone by since my brother and I had left Vienna. We checked into the Hotel Stefanie, a pleasant hotel with a very friendly staff.

We arranged a taxi to the Jewish cemetery. With the help of the cemetery office, the taxi driver and two gravediggers, we finally located the graves of my parents. As I stood there reflecting on their difficult lives and their early death, some of the long-carried sorrow left me. Perhaps G-d in his mercy had let them die before their time, to spare them the horrors of the concentration camps.

The same taxi took us to the apartment building in the tenth district where I had lived as a boy. We were the only Jews then living in the building of 45 apartments. I took some pictures and walked to the entrance.

An old man had been watching me and suddenly he gripped my arm and said: "You once lived on the third floor." He told me what had happened to most of the people—who was killed in the war, who had moved away, but most important, he assured me that he was never a Nazi.

On the way back to the hotel, the taxi driver talked about all the problems of Vienna and I could tell that he wanted to ask me how did I come to speak such good German and why did I leave. I was not in the mood to discuss it with him.

The next day we were real tourists. We walked along the pedestrian mall of the Rotenturmstrasse and the very fashionable Kärntner Straße. The streets were perfectly clean and full of well-dressed and happy people. It was apparent that Vienna was a prosperous city.

The storekeepers were very polite and friendly and, whether we bought anything or not, thanked us for coming into their store and asked us to enjoy our stay in Vienna. We asked a young man the way to the museum; he told us that it was a long way, and he insisted taking us in his car.

Many of the Vienna newspapers were if anything rather pro-Israel. At that time, they were discussing whether it was a good idea for Simon Wiesenthal to continue his search for war criminals. There were many letters to the editor. One, written by a lady, probably told the whole story: I am a strong supporter of Israel, I always buy Jaffa oranges because I want Israel to be strong so that the Jews don't come back to Vienna.

On Saturday morning we went to the synagogue near the Judengasse (Street of the Jews). It is marked on the map of Vienna as the state synagogue. The young guide-guard at the door made us check our camera—no picture-taking for security reasons. The synagogue is Orthodox and all the women sat upstairs.

I spoke to a few of the older men, hoping to get some information about a member of our family that may have survived the war. One man said to me, "Why do you people come here looking for survivors? Everyone is gone. There is nobody left." He was very disturbed to be reminded of the past. All the men had something in common—empty eyes that had seen the horrible past and could not see any hope for the future. After the service, a small group of tourists were having a discussion outside the synagogue. A woman from Warsaw told us that after 40 years she just had to visit Vienna. A young woman from Israel was visiting her mother, who did not want to leave Vienna. A young Austrian Jew told us that the few young Austrian Jews left in Vienna would not last long. He and his wife were leaving shortly for Israel. This, then, was what was left of the 200,000 Jews of Vienna—a mere 7,000 old and broken humans receiving a small pension from the Austrian government. In a few years' time one of Hitler's wishes would finally come true. Vienna will be judenrein—free of Jews.

We decided to splurge and have lunch at the Hotel Imperial. The service and the food were excellent, and so was the bill. After lunch we continued our walk along the Ringstrasse (the Vienna Ring Road) and over the bridge into the second district. Malzgasse Shiffgasse Herminengasse—this is where most of Vienna's 200,000 Jews lived before the war, and this is also where I spent the last six months before leaving Vienna.

Here were the great houses of learning—temples and the Polish Synagogue with its world-famous choir, where once Josef "Yossele" Rosenblatt performed. This is also where I spent the most terrifying night of my life. November 9–10, 1938—Kristallnacht, literally "Crystal Night," the Night of Broken Glass. The afternoon and evening papers had that day carried banner headlines: A Jew had shot a German diplomat in Paris. I remember that I hurried home as it was getting dark. The only one in the apartment was my brother.

Soon we heard the smashing of glass and screams as furniture and sometimes people were thrown out the windows. I remember the smoke and glow in the sky as all over Vienna the synagogues were burning. As if to shut out the world, we hid under the bed. Screams in our building and soon the sound of jackboots on our floor. The door was smashed open and we were dragged from our hiding place and made to join a large group of Jews already in the streets. We were made to carry placards reading "We are Jew pigs and do not deserve to live." We ended up in a large hall where we had to show our papers at various tables. As we proceeded, we were kicked and beaten; my brother and I were told to leave the hall by the left door. I noticed that most others left through another exit. Our door led to the streets of Vienna. My brother said, "Grüß Gott"—the Austrian greeting for "G-d be with you." At the door, the five young men with swastika armbands beat and kicked us, yelling "We have no G-d in Vienna, Hitler is our Fuhrer." The day after, we learned that all who were in the hall, with only a few exceptions, were deported to the Polish border and left to their fate.

The next morning our tour left Vienna. The drive through the Alps to Salzburg and Innsbruck was breathtakingly beautiful. That night as we sat in a crowded beer cellar, singing songs of all nations to the cheers of all present, I realized how easy it is to forget, even for us, the survivors. However, I resolved to visit Austria again, especially Vienna. It is so beautiful, friendly, and pleasant.

During a coffee stop the next day, I picked up a Vienna newspaper. On the second page, I noticed a picture of three gravestones with anti-Jewish Nazi slogans, and below it an article explaining that over the weekend, the Vienna State Synagogue, two other Jewish buildings and twenty gravestones in the Jewish Cemetery had been defaced with anti-Jewish Nazi slogans....

AGAIN? Or STILL?

Acknowledgements

This memoir was dictated by Martin Maxwell to his wife, Eleanor Maxwell, starting in 2018 up to his passing in December 2020. His grandson, Harris Maxwell, transcribed and edited the handwritten manuscript as well as coordinated with Centennial College Press on the publication of the work. Thankfully, many of Martin's presentations over the years were recorded, as well as a survivor testimony filmed in 1995 by Steven Spielberg's USC Shoah Foundation, which helped to fill in some details. Many of these recordings, published articles, and other information can be found at www.captmartinmaxwell.com.

Many thanks to Centennial College Press and especially to David Stover for publishing the book. Gratefully appreciated is the encouragement and devoted friendship of our late beloved friend Dr. Major Ken Hedges, who wrote the foreword.

Thanks also to Jory Brentjens, Conservator at the Airborne Museum in Hartenstein, for memorializing Martin's story and uniform as part of a permanent exhibit centred around the Battle of Arnhem. The shadow box that houses Martin's uniform was expertly assembled by Gary Brown at House of 10,000 Picture Frames & Art, who went above and beyond to ensure that the result was perfect.

A special thank you to Richard Jopson, the photographer who included Martin as part of his Arnhem Boys project and his exhibition at the Airborne Museum in Berlin. Through his photos we remember Martin as he was in his later years, full of life and a source of unlimited optimism.

We also wish to thank Ludmila Schnaider, who featured Martin as part of her project entitled "My Dear Veterans." Ludmila's work with Toronto-based veterans has been featured in many public spaces, including Toronto City Hall, and was made into a documentary with TLN Media Group.

We would be remiss in not mentioning Jesse and Maurice Webber, who adopted Martin and welcomed him with open arms into their family. Their son Laurie had two sons of his own, Anthony and Jonathan, who (with their wives Bernice and Nicky) have instilled essential human values into their children and grandchildren.

We would also like to recognize the Kindertransport organization sponsored by Rabbi Schonfeld in Britain, along with the Quakers and Prime Minister Winston Churchill. Without their efforts, Martin and his siblings likely would never have made it out of Austria.

Thank you to John Tory (former mayor of Toronto), who honoured Martin many times by including him in various ceremonies, as well as Rabbi Flanzreich and Cantor Eric Moses of Beth Sholom Synagogue, and the many friends who always provided encouragement and support. We also wish to thank the many employees and partners of National Home Products over the years, who took care of the business when Martin was out of the office educating young people and adults about the horrors of World War II.

Finally, a note of gratitude to Martin and Eleanor's sons Randy and Brian for all of their unwavering support for this project over the years. For examples of their unique talents: Randy wrote the obituary and the words for Martin's stone, and Brian wrote a piece of original music that he and his wife Wendy performed at Martin's memorial.

For Your Tomorrow, We Gave Our Today

Obituary

MAXWELL, Martin (Max Meisels) – Peacefully in his 97th year at Sunnybrook Health Sciences Centre after a valiant battle, his last, on Thursday, December 3, 2020.

Captain (Retired) Martin Maxwell, beloved husband of Eleanor. Devoted father and father-in-law of Randy and Vivian Maxwell and Brian and Wendy Maxwell.

Loving Zaidy Max to his grandchildren Harris Maxwell and Trisha Nakagawa, Carly and Jakob Marszowski, Bram Maxwell, Perri Maxwell and Michael Chaikof, and Loni Maxwell and Trevor Grohman, and great-grandfather of Nicole, Zoe and Lauren Marszowski.

Special uncle to Ruthy Kaiser, Allan Lunenfeld and Loraine St Louis, Susy Lunenfeld and Hector Nunez, Aron Posen, and Lauren Posen and Jason Cherney. Great-uncle of Jonathan Kaiser and Connor Sullivan and Jeffrey Kaiser and Peter Murphy, Emi Nunez and Eren Nunez. Brother-in-law to Elliott and Rachelle Posen.

Loving brother and brother-in-law to the late Berta and Joe Lunenfeld, the late Leo and Luba Majzels, and the late Josephine Meisels and Erna Meisels.

After the Nazis invaded Austria in 1938, Martin was evacuated to England on the Kindertransport, which offered safe haven to Jewish children. He was adopted as a son by the Webbers, a Jewish family in Manchester, and always remained close with their descendants.

In England, once he came of age, Martin joined Britain's Army Air Corps and trained as a glider pilot. A few days before the D-Day invasion, he was encouraged by a high-ranking officer to change his birth name from Max Meisels to Martin Maxwell to conceal his Jewish identity, were he to be captured.

At age 21, Martin flew a glider plane during D-Day in Normandy, France, bringing reinforcements to the soldiers who had captured

Pegasus bridge the night before, and then defending it for the following two days.

Three months later he flew into battle again, this time at Arnhem, Holland, where, after safely landing troops he was wounded and captured. As a POW he was to witness Nazi atrocities. Martin was liberated at the end of the war in May 1945.

Following Germany's capitulation on V-E Day, May 8, 1945, he was tasked, as a German-speaking British officer, with investigations in Washington, D.C., relating to war crimes.

Martin retired from the Army Air Corps with the rank of Captain. He was awarded some of the highest honours, including the Queen Elizabeth II Diamond Jubilee Medal and the Legion of Honour from France.

He has been involved in numerous community organizations including B'nai Brith and Jewish War Veterans of Canada. Eleanor was always by his side.

In referring to the millions of soldiers killed in the Second World War, Martin often quoted a famous inscription: "Tell them of us and say: For your tomorrow, we gave our today."

Heartfelt thanks to Dr. Steven Shumak, Dr. William Silverstein and the extended team members at Sunnybrook Health Sciences Centre for providing world class care, comfort and respect to "Max."

Donations in Martin's memory can be made to the Sarah and Chaim Neuberger Holocaust Education Centre of Toronto (416-631-5689, neuberger@ujafed.org), or to a charity of your choice.

He's in Our Hearts

There is a light that touched us all
It make us glow, it makes us tall
It comes from Dad, he made us shine
From generosity, he was so kind

For Your Tomorrow, We Gave Our Today

Without a thought, now from above
He gave of himself and with so much love
And always thinking, a mind so clear
Although he's gone, he's always here

From desperate times and broken dreams
Emerged a man (whose life, it seems) was to
Have a heart, that beat beyond his own
To have a life, a wife, a home

We always remember, his humour, his pride
He'll be with us always, deep inside
But most of all, the times we had
You've touched our hearts … we love you Dad

Written by Lewis Brian Maxwell
SOCAN Registration # A2644766
Registration Date: December 5, 2020

A Selection of Photographs and Documents

Family picture taken in Vienna.
Father Abraham Meisels
(standing); Max Meisels, age 6
(left); mother Rachel Meisels; baby
Berta; Erna, age 4; Josephine, age 5
(right).

Restored family grave for Martin's parents in Vienna.

Left: Martin's brother Leo Majzels, around age 18.
Right: Martin as a young man.

For Your Tomorrow, We Gave Our Today

Martin's sister, Berta Meisels Lunenfeld.

Martin's adoptive parents, Maurice and Jessie Webber.

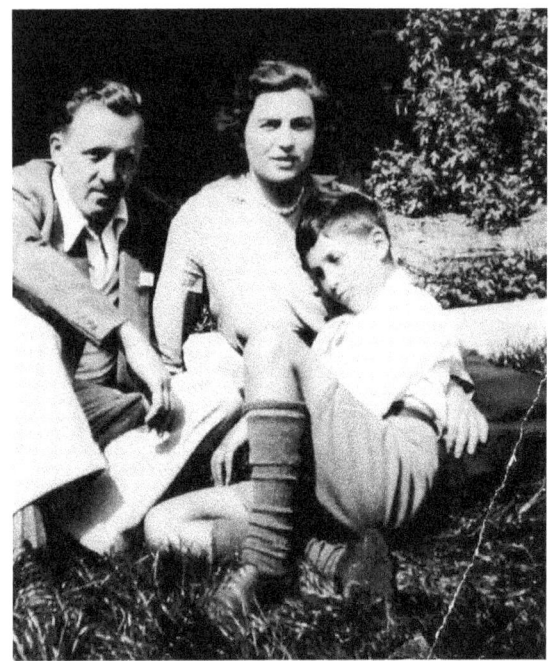

Martin's adoptive mother, Jessie Webber (centre), with Ben Morris (left; husband of Jessie's sister) and Jessie's son Laurie Webber (right; age 10½ in this photograph).

Martin in 1942. "Soccer played a major role in my life, and in army and public life."

Martin as a sergeant in the British Army, with friends.

Brother Leo Majzels, bombardier and flight engineer in the U.S. Army Air Force, 1943, "somewhere in Italy," according to the inscription on the back of the photo.

A card given to Martin Maxwell by the leader of the prisoner of war camp where he served after the war. The outside of the card is reproduced above.

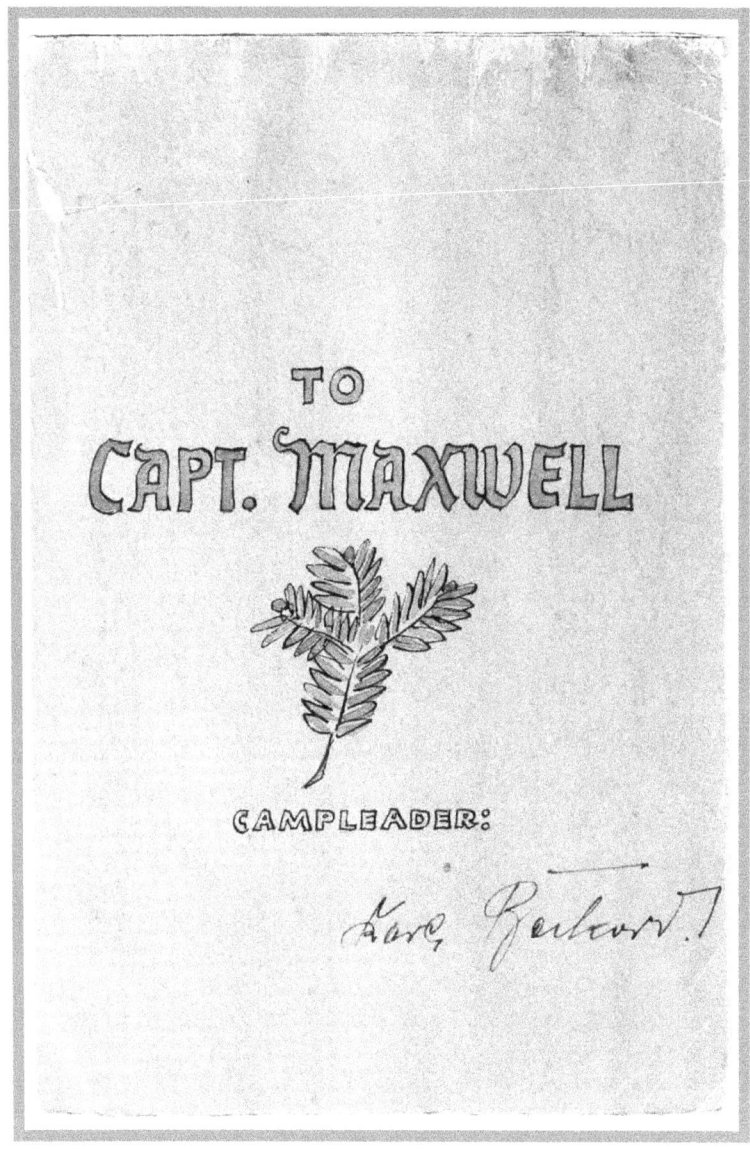

Inside of the card given to Martin Maxwell by the leader of the prisoner of war camp. The card was signed by the camp leader.

Pegasus Bridge, June 12, 1944. The night before D-Day, an operation was launched to capture two bridges over the Orne River, Pegasus Bridge (seen above) and what came to be called "Horsa Bridge," just to the east. The operation's purpose was to protect the eastern flank of Allied landings at Sword Beach by cutting off German armoured forces. Six Horsa gliders were launched from England. Five of them landed just after midnight close to Pegasus Bridge, while the sixth landed about eleven kilometres away near a bridge crossing the River Dives. The surprise attack resulted in Pegasus Bridge's rapid capture by the Allies with only two fatalities. Early in the morning of June 6, Allied paratroopers reinforced the troops who had initially captured the bridge. The photograph above was taken by a Sergeant Christie of the No. 5 [British] Army Film and Photographic Unit. (Photograph B5288, Imperial War Museum Collection via Wikimedia Commons).

Army Form O 1651.

| This Notice should be carefully preserved and should accompany any enquiry | The COMMISSIONERS of INCOME DUTY, THE WAR OFFICE, DROITWICH SPA, WORCS. | File No. 93 |

13106631   WS/SGT
MAXWELL M.
A.A.C

INCOME TAX

WAR OFFICE ASSESSMENT.

Year 1945-46, ending 5 April, 1946.

The particulars of the assessment made upon you for the year ending 5th April, 1946, are set out overleaf. Information regarding the amount of the official emoluments assessed may be obtained from me. Enquiries relating to current deductions of tax should be made to the Paymaster or Agent from whom you draw pay. Enquiries on other matters should be made to H.M. Inspector of Taxes (Departmental Claims Branch) at the address given below.

R. ROBERTSON;
for Clerk to the Commissioners

APPEALS.

You may, if you so desire, appeal to the Special Commissioners against the assessment in respect of your emoluments.

Notice of such appeal should be given in writing, quoting the above file number, to H.M. Inspector of Taxes (Departmental Claims Branch), The Hydro, Llandudno, Caernarvonshire, within 21 days of the receipt of this statement, and the grounds of your appeal should be stated.

(1052) 37128 24769/D6635 450M 8/45 SP/TBH Gp.25

First page of Martin Maxwell's British War Office tax form, 1945.

Martin Maxwell (right) in civilian clothes in Washington, D.C., while working on war crimes investigations, 1948.

Martin Maxwell (far left) with colleagues and friends in Washington, D.C., March 1949.

British Army release certificate for Martin Maxwell. He was granted 77 days' leave beginning November 1, 1949, then released from duty as of January 17, 1950.

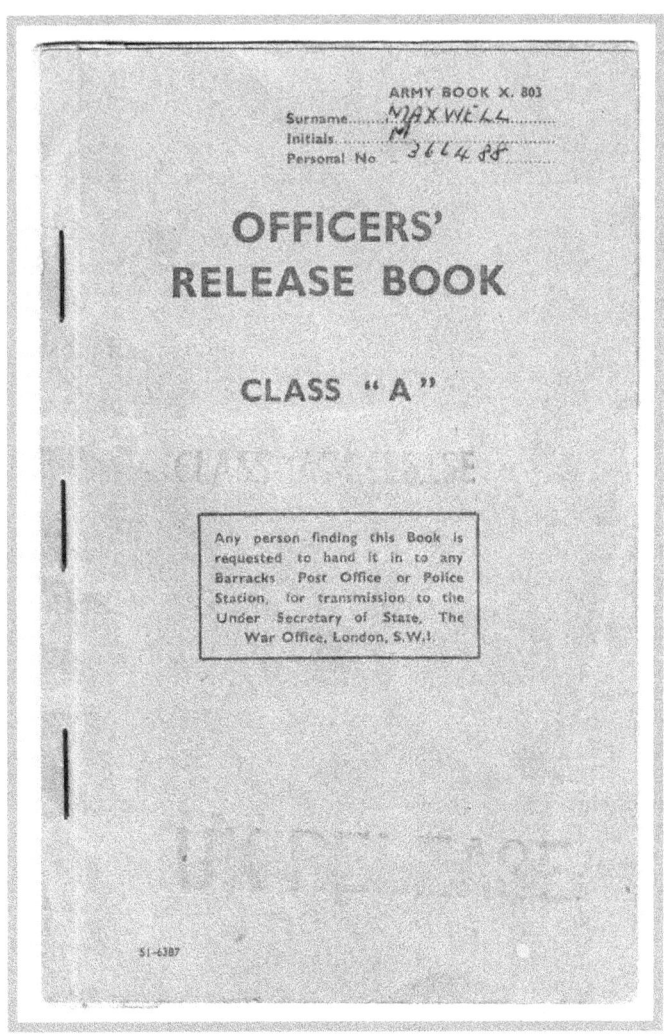

Cover of Martin Maxwell's "Officers' Release Book," retained by him after his release from service in 1950.

For Your Tomorrow, We Gave Our Today

Inside page of Captain Maxwell's release book. He was granted 77 days' leave prior to his release from the Army on January 17, 1950.

```
Registered Office
203, Regent Street   London W.1.
Tele: Regent 5854( 5 lines)
                    The Manchester
       HADASSIAH              RESTAURANT
            Proprietors : Hesther Caterers Ltd.

Managing Director.
J.VILENSKI M.A.              CROMFORD HOUSE, CROMFORD COURT
     Director.               Off Market Street.MANCHESTER 4.
T.C.MOODY A.C.A.                Blackfriars 32024 9163.

                  TO WHOM IT MAY CONCERN.        May 25th 51.

       It is with regret that I learn that Mr. Martin
Maxwell, our Snackbar manager wishes to leave this
Restaurant.  During his employment here( August 20th-
to date ) I have found Mr. Maxwell to be very conscientious
loyal and honest.  He handled his staff well and has a very
pleasing manner.  I consider him an asset to any establish-
ment, and I therefore highly recommend him to any future
employer

                      Signed:     W.Geller.

                                  _____

                                  W.Geller.    Manager
```

Reference letter for Martin Maxwell, written by W. Geller, manager of the Manchester Hadassiah Restaurant, May 25, 1951.

For Your Tomorrow, We Gave Our Today

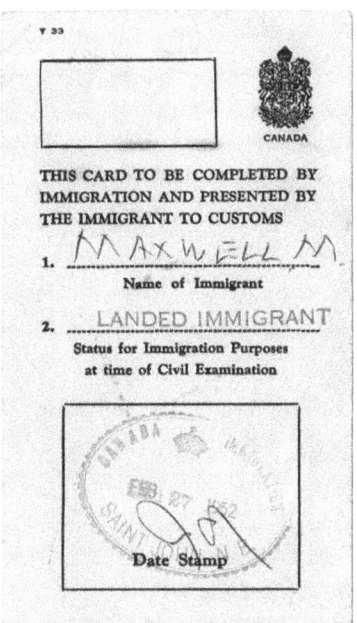

Martin Maxwell's immigration card, stamped by the Canadian government's immigration department in Saint John, New Brunswick, on February 27, 1952.

Martin Maxwell worked for Lever Bros. in the 1950's. Here he is making a call at a drugstore in 1957.

Reunion with the Webber family in Southport, England, in September 1985. From left: Laurie Webber, Freda Webber, Jessie Webber, Maurice Webber ("Pops"), and Martin Maxwell.

Martin Maxwell in Holland in 2015 at the University of Utrecht. The school honoured Martin by naming the tree the Martin Maxwell Tree of Freedom, to remember him in case he could not come to ceremonies in 2020.

Martin Maxwell being interviewed in Holland in 2015.

Martin Maxwell remembering a friend during a visit to an Allied Cemetery.

Martin Maxwell and wife Eleanor at a Jewish war veterans event, likely in November 2019.

Martin Maxwell in 2018 wearing the jacket of his army summer uniform. (Photograph by Richard Jopson; https://richardjopson.com/arnhem-boys.)

Martin Maxwell in uniform. (Photograph by Richard Jopson.)

www.ingramcontent.com/pod-product-compliance
Lightning Source LLC
Chambersburg PA
CBHW050832010526
44110CB00054BA/2657